DK EYEWITNESS

T0001637

TOP10
PRAGUE

Top 10 Prague Highlights

The Top 10 of Everything

CONTENTS

Prague Area by Area

Streetsmart

Within each Top 10 list in this book, no hierarchy of quality or popularity is implied. All 10 are, in the editor's opinion, of roughly equal merit.

Title page, front cover and spine *Aerial view of the Church of Our Lady before Týn at sunset*
Back cover, clockwise from top left
The Astronomical Clock, Old Town Hall; shops lining a cobblestoned street; National Museum at Wenceslas Square; Church of Our Lady before Týn; grand Prague Castle and Charles Bridge

The rapid rate at which the world is changing is constantly keeping the DK Eyewitness team on our toes. While we've worked hard to ensure that this edition of Prague is accurate and up-to-date, we know that opening hours alter, standards shift, prices fluctuate, places close and new ones pop up in their stead. So, if you notice we've got something wrong or left something out, we want to hear about it. Please get in touch at **travelguides@dk.com**

Welcome to
Prague

The City of a Hundred Spires, with its medieval cityscape intact, continues to dazzle as it has for the better part of a millennium. The Old Town Hall's Astronomical Clock still chimes the hour as crowds cross the cobblestoned Charles Bridge under the gaze of the castle. With DK Eyewitness Top 10 Prague, this well-preserved city is yours to explore.

Praguers call their city Matka měst – the Mother of Cities – a reference to a time in the 14th century when Prague served as the capital of the Holy Roman Empire. Architectural treasures like **Prague Castle**, **St Vitus Cathedral** and **Loreta** testify to that former grandeur. But Prague is more than pretty buildings. The city of Dvořák, Kafka, Bedřich Smetana and Václav Havel still throbs with culture, music, literature, theatre – and intrigue. All who visit are bewitched by the spires and the cobbles, the shadows and the tiny lanes of the most enchanting city in Central Europe.

And did we mention the beer? The Czech Republic prides itself as the home of the world's finest lager. What could be better than winding through the Baroque streetscape of **Malá Strana**, taking in the National Gallery's collection of modern art at the **Trade Fair Palace** and enjoying the green spaces of the **Wallenstein Garden** or **Petřín Hill** and then retiring to a traditional pub like **U Zlatého tygra** to digest it all over a mug of Pilsner Urquell or Staropramen?

Whether you're visiting for a weekend or a week, our Top 10 guide is brings together the best of everything that Prague has to offer, from the bustle of the **New Town** and the imperial flavour of **Hradčany** to the Gothic splendour of the **Old Town** and the understated grace of the former Jewish quarter of **Josefov**. The guide has useful tips throughout, from seeking out what's free to places off the beaten track, plus eight easy-to-follow itineraries, designed to tie together a clutch of sights in a short space of time. Add inspiring photography and detailed maps, and you've got the essential pocket-sized travel companion. **Enjoy the book, and enjoy Prague**.

Clockwise from top: **Charles Bridge, Wenceslas Square, Spanish Synagogue, Wallenstein Garden, fresco at Loreta, stained glass at St Vitus Cathedral, aerial view of the city**

Exploring Prague

There is a wealth of things to see and do in Prague. Whether you're here just for the weekend or have the luxury of a couple of extra days, these two- and four-day itineraries will help you to plan your time and make the most of your visit.

Charles Bridge links the Old Town and Malá Strana quarters of Prague.

Two Days in Prague

Day ❶
MORNING
Marvel at the **Old Town Square** (see pp18–21), taking in the Astronomical Clock. Ramble through tiny lanes towards **Charles Bridge** (see pp22–3).
AFTERNOON
Meander through **Malá Strana** (see pp92–9), pausing at St Nicholas Church (see p94). Hike up **Nerudova** (see p93) – note the house signs (see pp52–3) – to **Prague Castle** (see pp12–15), where you can tour the Old Royal Palace and St Vitus Cathedral (see pp16–17).

Day ❷
MORNING
Begin at **Josefov** (see pp108–13) and the **Jewish Museum** (see p49). Don't miss the **Old Jewish Cemetery** (see pp28–31). The **St Agnes of Bohemia Convent** (see pp34–5) nearby houses the National Gallery's medieval art.
AFTERNOON
Visit bustling **Wenceslas Square** (see pp36–7), the heart of the New Town

Astronomical Clock

(see pp114–21). Admire the **National Museum** (see p118) before walking down Narodní towards the river to the **National Theatre** (see p66).

Four Days in Prague

Day ❶
MORNING
Visit the **Powder Gate** and **Municipal House** (see p85) before making your way to the **Old Town Square** (see pp18–21). Then stroll to **Charles Bridge** (see pp22–3).
AFTERNOON
Wander through **Malá Strana** (see pp92–9) via **Nerudova** (see p93) to **Prague Castle** (see pp12–15) and its Old Royal Palace, **St Vitus Cathedral** (see pp16–17) and Golden Lane.

Day ❷
MORNING
Spend time at the **Jewish Museum** (see p49), focusing on the **Old Jewish**

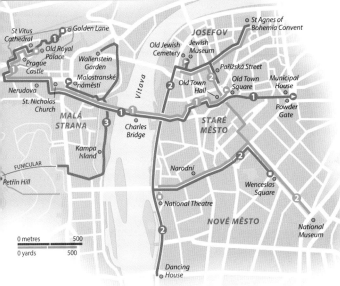

The Wallenstein Garden is free for the public to enter, and hosts various cultural events during the summer.

Cemetery (see pp28–31). Explore exclusive Pařížská street then stop by the **St Agnes of Bohemia Convent** (see pp34–5) for its collection of medieval art.

AFTERNOON
Head to the river and walk south along it to the **National Theatre** (see p66) and the **Dancing House** (see p116). Then take stately Národní to **Wenceslas Square** (see pp36–7).

Day ❸
MORNING
Start at **Malostranské náměstí** (see p94). Amble through **Kampa Island** (see p94) and **Wallenstein Garden** (see p79). Make for **Petřín Hill** (see pp38–9) and ride the funicular up.

AFTERNOON
From Petřín, head to **Strahov Monastery** (see p38) and to **Loreta** (see pp26–7). Be sure to stroll along tranquil **Nový Svět** (see p102).

Day ❹
MORNING
View the National Gallery's modern and contemporary art at the **Trade Fair Palace** (see pp32–3). Then admire the exhibition grounds at **Výstaviště** (the interiors are currently closed for renovation) or enjoy a walk at nearby **Stromovka** (see p124).

AFTERNOON
Explore **Vyšehrad**, the city's spiritual home (see p123). Visit the **Slavín Monument, Casemates** and **Sts Peter and Paul Cathedral** (see p127).

Top 10 Prague Highlights

Historic buildings in Prague's Old Town Square

🔟 **Prague Highlights**

At the heart of Europe, Prague's beautiful cityscape – from the Gothic exuberance of its castle and cathedral to the dignity of the medieval Jewish Cemetery and the 19th-century opulence of the "new" town – has been created and sustained by emperors, artists and religious communities. Under Communist rule, Prague was off the tourist map, but since 1989 the Czech capital has seen a surge of visitors eager to take in this spectacular city.

1 Prague Castle

Visitors can spend a day exploring this hilltop fortress of the Přemyslids, now home to the Czech president (see pp12–15).

2 St Vitus Cathedral

The glory of the castle complex, St Vitus took nearly 600 years to build. Don't miss the exquisite stained glass and delightful gargoyles (see pp16–17).

3 Old Town Square

The city has few finer charms than watching the moon rise over the Old Town Square between the towers of the Church of Our Lady before Týn (see pp18–21).

5 Loreta

Pilgrims have visited this Baroque shrine to the Virgin Mary since the 17th century. Visitors can admire the priceless ornaments held in its treasury (see pp26–7).

4 Charles Bridge

The huge crowds can make it hard to appreciate the beautiful statues on this bridge that links the city's two halves, but a visit is a must when in Prague (see pp22–3).

7 Trade Fair Palace

One of Europe's first Functionalist buildings, the Trade Fair Palace now houses the National Gallery's collection of modern art (see pp32–3).

6 Old Jewish Cemetery

This jumble of tombstones in the former Jewish ghetto gives little indication of the number of people buried here (see pp28–31).

8 St Agnes of Bohemia Convent

The oldest Gothic building in the city is home to the National Gallery's collection of medieval art (see pp34–5).

9 Wenceslas Square

From a humble horse market, the square has grown into a modern hub, with monuments recalling its role in the nation's history (see pp36–7).

10 Petřín Hill

Perched above Malá Strana, the hill is crisscrossed with footpaths offering some of the city's best views. The Ukrainian church is wonderfully romantic (see pp38–9).

🔟 ⭐ Prague Castle

Crowned by St Vitus Cathedral, Prague Castle *(Pražský hrad)* is the metaphorical and historical throne of the Czech lands. Around 880 CE, Prince Bořivoj built a wooden fortress on this hilltop above the river, establishing it as the dynastic base of the Přemyslids. In the 14th century the castle became the seat of the Holy Roman Empire. Much of it was rebuilt by Empress Maria Theresa in the latter half of the 18th century, giving it a formal Neo-Classical look. Today the castle is the official residence of the Czech president.

1 Old Royal Palace
While Prince Bořivoj made do with a wooden structure, subsequent residences were built on top of each other as the tastes of Bohemia's rulers changed *(see p14)*. Halls are decorated with coats of arms **(above)**.

2 South Gardens
Emperor Ferdinand I and his son Maximilian II gave the castle some greenery in the late 16th century, and First Republic architect Josip Plečnik created the lined paths, steps and grottoes that extend to Malá Strana.

3 White Tower
The castle's White Tower was once used as a prison and torture chamber. Today, shops here sell grisly souvenirs. The gangways from which archers once watched over the moat are lined with replicas of weapons.

4 Lobkowicz Palace
The only privately owned building **(below)** in the castle complex, this rival to the National Gallery holds works by Bruegel, Canaletto, Dürer, Rubens and Velázquez in its collection.

Prague Castle and the Vltava

5 St George's Convent
Prince Boleslav II, with Princess Mlada, established the first Czech convent for Benedictine nuns here in 973 CE. The Romanesque building is not open to the public.

6 St George's Basilica
Prince Vratislav built the basilica around 920 CE. The 13th-century chapel of St Ludmila, St Wenceslas's grandmother, is decorated with beautiful 16th-century paintings **(above)**.

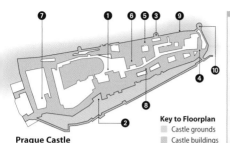

Prague Castle

Key to Floorplan
- Castle grounds
- Castle buildings

CASTLE GUIDE

Most of the grounds are free to enter, but tickets to see the interiors are sold at the information centres in the second and third courtyards. Standard tickets include entrance to the Old Royal Palace, St George's Basilica, St Vitus Cathedral and Golden Lane (including Daliborka Tower). You can add on the Great South Tower and The Story of Prague Castle *(see p14)* exhibition for extra fees.

8 Rosenberg Palace

This 16th-century palace has had multiple uses: as an 18th-century residence for noble-women, as part of the Ministry of Internal Affairs of Czechoslovakia and as modern presidential offices.

9 Golden Lane

In order to avoid paying guild dues in town, goldsmiths lived in these colourful little houses **(below)** that were built into the castle walls.

7 Chapel of the Holy Cross

Built by the Italian architect Anselmo Lurago in 1763, this chapel **(left)** is usually closed, but you can still admire the statues of St Peter and St Paul on the façade.

10 Daliborka Tower

When captured, Dalibor, a Czech Robin Hood figure, became the first prisoner of the tower that now takes his name.

NEED TO KNOW

MAP C2 ▪ Hradčany
▪ 224 372423, 224 372434
▪ Adm (various combination tickets available; under 6s free; audio guides available)
▪ www.hrad.cz

Prague Castle buildings (Old Royal Palace, St George's Basilica, Golden Lane & Daliborka Tower): open 9am–5pm daily

Great South Tower: open Apr–Oct: 9am–6pm daily (Nov–Mar: to 5pm)

Lobkowicz Palace: open 10am–6pm daily; www.lobkowicz.cz

Grounds: open 6am–10pm daily

▪ The change of guard ceremony happens on the hour and at noon in the first courtyard.

Old Royal Palace Features

Vaulted ceiling of the Vladislav Hall

1 Vladislav Hall

Here, Benedikt Rejt created a mastery of Gothic design with the elaborate vaulting. It has been used for coronations and jousting tournaments, and, since the First Republic, the country's presidents have been ceremoniously sworn in here.

2 Louis Wing

Only ten years and a few steps separate the southern wing from the main hall, but in that brief space, Rejt moved castle architecture from Gothic to Renaissance. Bohemian nobles met here in an administrative body when the king was away.

3 Bohemian Chancellery

Protestant noblemen threw two Catholic governors and their secretary from the east window, sparking off the Thirty Years' War. Their fall was broken by a dung heap – or an intervening angel, depending on who you ask.

4 Old Land Rolls Room

The coats of arms on the walls belong to clerks who tracked property ownership and court decisions from 1614 to 1777. Until Maria Theresa, records were unnumbered, identified only by elaborate covers.

5 Riders' Staircase

The low steps and vaulted ceiling of this stairway permitted mounted knights to make grand entrances to the spectacular jousting tournaments held in Vladislav Hall.

6 Chapel of All Saints

A door leads from Vladislav Hall to a balcony above the Chapel of All Saints, modelled by Petr Parléř on Paris's Gothic Sainte-Chapelle. After fire destroyed it in 1541, it was redesigned in Renaissance style. Of particular artistic note is Hans van Aachen's *Triptych of the Angels*.

7 Soběslav Residence

Prince Soběslav built the first stone palace in the 12th century.

8 The Story of Prague Castle

This informative and entertaining exhibition covers the history, events, personalities and arts and crafts relating to the main castle complex.

9 Busts from Petr Parléř's Workshop

These impressive effigies, created in the late 14th century, include the grandfather-father-grandson set of John of Luxembourg, Charles IV and Wenceslas IV.

10 Diet

Bohemian nobles met the king here in a prototype parliament. The king sat on the throne (the one seen today is a 19th-century replica), the archbishop sat on his right, while the estates sat on his left. The portraits on the wall show, from the left, Maria Theresa, her husband Franz, Josef II, Leopold II and Franz I, who fought Napoleon at Austerlitz.

The stately Diet hall

PRAGUE'S DEFENESTRATIONS

Prague's first recorded instance of execution by hurling the condemned people from a window occurred at the outset of the Hussite Wars in 1419. Vladislav II's officials met a similar fate in 1483. Perhaps as a tribute to their forebears, more than 100 Protestant nobles stormed the Old Royal Palace in 1618 and cast two hated Catholic governors and their secretary out of the window. Protestants said the men's fall was broken by a dung heap swept from the Vladislav Hall after a recent tournament, while Catholics claimed they were saved by angels. The incident is often cited as the spark that began the Thirty Years' War. After the defeat of the Protestants by the army of the Holy Roman Emperor Ferdinand II at the first skirmish at White Mountain *(see p42)*, 27 of these nobles were executed in the Old Town Square *(see pp18–21)*.

**TOP 10
RULERS OF PRAGUE**

1 Wenceslas (around 907–935)

2 Ottokar II (1233–78)

3 Charles IV (1316–78)

4 Wenceslas IV (1361–1419)

5 Rudolf II (1552–1612)

6 Tomáš Garrigue Masaryk (1850–1937)

7 Edvard Beneš (1884–1948)

8 Gustáv Husák (1913–1991)

9 Václav Havel (1936–2011)

10 Václav Klaus (b 1941)

The Battle of White Mountain (Bílá Hora) in 1620 played a role in the Counter-Reformation and the re-Catholization of the Czech lands.

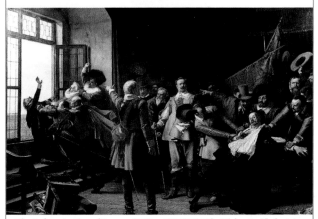

The Defenestration of Prague, 23 May 1618 **(1889)** by Václav Brožík depicts the Protestants' attack on the Catholic governors. Painted 271 years after the event, it illustrates how the event remained in the Czech consciousness.

🔟 ⭐ St Vitus Cathedral

The spectacular Gothic *Katedrála svatého Víta* is an unmissable sight in Prague, not least because of its dominant position on Hradčany hill, looming over the Vltava and the rest of the city. Prince Wenceslas first built a rotunda here on a pagan worship site and dedicated it to St Vitus *(svatý Vít)*, a Roman saint. Matthew d'Arras began work on the grand cathedral in 1344 when Prague was named an archbishopric. He died shortly thereafter and Charles IV hired the Swabian wunderkind Petr Parléř to take over. With the intervention of the Hussite Wars, however, work stopped and, remarkably, construction was only finally completed in 1929.

1 Great South Tower

The point at which the Hussite Wars halted construction of this 96-m (315-ft) tower is clear. When work resumed, architectural style had moved into the Renaissance, hence the rounded cap on a Gothic base **(left)**.

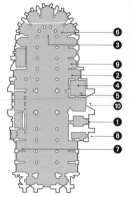

2 Royal Crypt

The greatest kings of Bohemia are buried in a single room beneath the cathedral, including Charles IV, Wenceslas IV and Rudolf II.

St Vitus Cathedral

3 High Altar

Bounded by St Vitus Chapel and the marble sarcophagi of Ferdinand I and family, the high altar and chancel follow a strict Neo-Gothic philosophy **(above)**.

4 Wenceslas Chapel

This stands on the site of the first rotunda and contains St Wenceslas's tomb **(right)**. The frescoes of Christ's Passion on the lower wall are surrounded by 1,300 semi-precious stones. To celebrate his son Ludvik's coronation, Vladislav II commissioned the upper frescoes of St Wenceslas's life.

7 New Archbishop's Chapel

Czech artists Alfons Mucha created the Art Nouveau window of the Slavic saints for the chapel **(left)**. Despite appearances, the glass is painted, not stained.

5 Bohemian Crown Jewels

You'd think there would be a safer place for the crown and sceptre of Bohemia, but the coronation chamber of Wenceslas Chapel is said to be guarded by the spirit of the saint.

PETR PARLÉŘ

After the death of Matthew d'Arras, Charles IV made the Swabian Petr Parléř his chief architect. Parléř undertook work on St Vitus Cathedral, Charles Bridge and numerous other Gothic monuments. He trained numerous artisans, and his talented sons and nephews continued his work after his death in 1399.

8 Sigismund

One of four Renaissance bells in the Great South Tower, the 18-tonne bell affectionately known as Sigismund is the nation's largest and dates from 1549. It takes four volunteers to ring the bell on important church holidays and at events.

9 Royal Oratory

The royals crossed a narrow bridge from the Old Royal Palace *(see p12)* to this private gallery for Mass. The coats of arms represent all the countries ruled by Vladislav II.

6 The Tomb of St John of Nepomuk

The silver for this 1,680-kg (3,700-lb) coffin came from the Bohemian mining town Kutná Hora, signified by the miners' statues to the left of the tomb.

10 Golden Portal

This triple-arched arcade **(above)** was the main entrance to the cathedral until the western end was completed in the 20th century.

NEED TO KNOW

MAP C2 ■ Third Courtyard, Prague Castle ■ 224 372423/34 (castle information centres) ■ Adm (only combined tickets with the castle available at the information centres in the castle courtyards; South Tower costs extra) ■ www. katedralasvate hovita.cz

Cathedral: open 9am–5pm Mon–Sat, noon–5pm Sun (Nov–Mar: to 4pm)

Great South Tower: open 10am–6pm daily (Nov–Mar: to 5pm)

■ The entrance (western) areas of St Vitus Cathedral can be visited for free – you'll see about a quarter of the building. Admission is charged for other areas.

■ The Royal Crypt may be entered with a guide, and you can see the basilica.

TOP 10 ★ Old Town Square

As the heart and soul of the city, the Old Town Square *(Staroměstské náměstí)* is hard to miss. There was a marketplace here in the 11th century, but it was in 1338, when John of Luxembourg gave Prague's burghers permission to form a town council, that the Old Town Hall was built and the square came into its own. Today, it has a lively atmosphere, with café tables set out in front of painted façades, hawkers selling their wares and horse-drawn carriages waiting to ferry tourists around.

1 Dům u Minuty

The "House at the Minute" **(below)** probably takes its name from the not-so-minute *sgraffito* images on its walls. The alchemical symbols adorning Staroměstské náměstí 2 date from 1610. Writer Franz Kafka *(see p50)* lived in the black-and-white house as a boy, from 1889 to 1896.

Prague's beautiful Old Town Square

2 House at the Stone Bell

Formerly done up in Baroque style, workers discovered the Gothic façade of this house as late as 1980. On the southwestern corner is the bell which gives the house its name. The Municipal Gallery often hosts temporary exhibitions here.

3 Church of Our Lady before Týn

This Gothic edifice **(right)** began as a humble church *(see p45)* serving residents in the mercantile town *(týn)* in the 14th century. Following architectural customs of the time, the south tower is stouter than the north one; they are said to depict Adam and Eve.

4 St Nicholas Cathedral

Prague has two Baroque churches of St Nicholas, both built by Kilian Ignac Dientzenhofer. The architect completed the one, called the cathedral now, in Old Town **(above)** two years before starting Malá Strana's *(see p94)*. Regular concerts *(see p67)* here are worth a visit.

Jan Hus Memorial

Hus was burned at the stake in 1415 for proposing radical church reform. The inscription below the figure of Hus **(right)** at the 1915 memorial reads "Truth Will Prevail".

JAN HUS

The rector of Prague (later Charles) University, Jan Hus was dedicated to fighting against corruption in the church. Declared a heretic by the church, he was summoned to Germany and was burned at the stake. Czech resentment turned into civil war, with Hussite rebels facing the power of Rome. But the Hussites split into moderate and radical factions, the former defeating the latter in 1434. Hus is still a national figure – 6 July, the day he was killed, is a public holiday.

⑦ Ungelt

The courtyard behind Týn church was home to foreign merchants in the 14th century, but today it houses smart boutiques and cafés.

⑩ Štorch House

At Staroměstské náměstí 16 **(left)**, the focal points are Art Nouveau paintings of St Wenceslas (the patron saint of Bohemia) and the three Magi.

⑥ Marian Column

On Czechoslovakia's declaration of independence in 1918, this former column reminded jubilant mobs of Habsburg rule and they tore it down. In 2020, the column was reconstructed.

⑧ Kinský Palace

This ornate Rococo palace now houses the National Gallery's temporary exhibitions *(see p48)*. It was once home to the haberdashery owned by Franz Kafka's father, Hermann.

Malé náměstí ⑨

The ornate wrought-iron well in the centre of the "Small Square" doubles as a plague memorial. The elaborate murals of crafters on the façade of Rott House **(right)** were designed by Mikoláš Aleš. From the 19th century to the early 1990s, the building was an ironmongery.

NEED TO KNOW

MAP M3 ◼ Old Town

Kinský Palace: Staroměstské náměstí 12
Old Town Hall: Staroměstské náměstí 1; 236 002629; Halls & Cellars: open 9am–7pm daily (from 11am Mon; Jan–Mar: from 10am); Tower: open 9am–9pm daily (from 11am Mon; Jan–Mar: 10am–8pm); adm (combined, family and reduced tickets available); www.staromestskaradnicepraha.cz

◼ Climbing on the Jan Hus Memorial or trampling the flowers could earn you a fine as well as embarrassment.

Old Town Hall Features

1 Astronomical Clock
During the day, bells ring, cocks crow and 15th-century statues dance on the hour while crowds of tourists watch from below.

Apostles in the Astronomical Clock

2 Apostles
Marionette artist Vojtěch Sucharda carved the 12 wooden figures that emerge from the clock every hour – they replace the ones destroyed by German artillery in 1945.

3 Art Gallery
On the Old Town Hall's ground floor is an exhibition space which features temporary shows.

4 Dukla Memorial
Behind a brass plaque marked with the year 1944 is a pot of soil from the Dukla battlefield. German artillery gunned down 84,000 Red Army soldiers in this Slovak pass in one of the most grievous military miscalculations of World War II.

Dukla Memorial

5 White Mountain Memorial
In the pavement on the town hall's eastern side are set 27 crosses in memory of the Bohemian nobles who were executed for their role in the Thirty Years' War. After the Battle of White Mountain (see p42), the men were publicly hanged, beheaded or drawn and quartered here.

6 Gothic Chapel
The small chapel adjoining the Mayors' Hall was consecrated in 1381 in honour of Sts Wenceslas, Vitus and Ludmila. Wenceslas IV's emblem and his wife Eufemia's initial adorn the entrance portal. In the nave is a model of the Marian column (see p19) which stood on the square until 1918 and was returned in 2020.

7 Elevator
The elevator to the viewing gallery of the tower won a design award in 1999. Oddly enough, its space-age design works harmoniously with the stony surroundings. It also permits wheelchair access to the top of the tower – a rare consideration in Prague.

8 Viewing Gallery
The parapet under the Old Town Hall's roof affords visitors a unique view of the square and the Old Town below. A little pocket change will buy you two minutes on a miniature telescope, with which you can admire the Prague Valley.

9 Gothic Cellars
The cellars of the Old Town Hall were once ground-floor rooms. The town was subject to flooding, so more earth was added to keep the burghers' feet dry. The spaces were used as granaries as well as debtors' prisons.

10 The Green
The Old Town Hall's north wing was severely damaged in an urban fight between the Germans and the Czechs during World War II. After the war, the wing was torn down. Now the area is lined with stalls selling Czech handicrafts.

BUILDING THE OLD TOWN HALL

Prague's Old Town received its charter and fortifications from John of Luxembourg in 1338, but its town clerk had to wait nearly 150 years for an office. The Old Town Hall was cobbled together from existing houses over the centuries until it comprised the five houses that stand at Staroměstské náměstí 1–2 today. The town hall's eastern wing once stretched to within a few feet of St Nicholas Cathedral *(see p18)*, but in 1945 German artillery bombardment reduced it to rubble. The 69.5-m (228-ft) tower was built in 1364, and in 1410 the imperial clockmaker Mikuláš of Kadaň created the basic mechanism of the Prague Orloj, or Astronomical Clock. In 1552 Jan Táborský was put in charge, and by 1566 the clock was fully mechanized.

TOP 10 FEATURES OF THE ASTRONOMICAL CLOCK

1 Solar clock
2 Lunar clock
3 Josef Mánes Calendar
4 Apostles
5 Angel and the Sciences
6 Vanity, Avarice, Death and Lust
7 Rooster
8 Hourly shows
9 Mikuláš of Kadaň
10 Dial

The Astronomical Clock not only tells the time, but also displays the movement of the sun and moon through the signs of the zodiac, and of the planets around the earth. The calendar plate below the clock has paintings by 19th-century Czech artist Josef Mánes.

TOP 10 ⭐ Charles Bridge

The spectacular Charles Bridge (*Karlův most*) has witnessed processions, battles, executions and, increasingly, film shoots since its construction between 1357 and 1402. Architect Petr Parléř built it in Gothic style to replace its predecessor, the Judith Bridge. The bridge's most distinguishing feature is its gallery of 30 statues. The religious figures were installed from 1683 onwards to lead people back to the church. Some, such as Bohn's Calvary, are politically controversial; others, such as Braun's St Luitgard, are incomparably lovely. Today all the statues are copies, with the originals preserved in museums across the city.

Old Town Bridge Tower ①

This beautiful Gothic tower, designed by Petr Parléř (see p17), was built at the end of the 14th century. Visitors can climb the 138 stairs to the viewing gallery for a jaw-dropping panoramic view of the city.

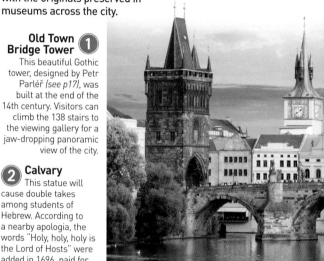

Charles Bridge and the Old Town bridge tower

② Calvary

This statue will cause double takes among students of Hebrew. According to a nearby apologia, the words "Holy, holy, holy is the Lord of Hosts" were added in 1696, paid for by a local Jewish man who had been accused of profaning the cross.

③ The Lorraine Cross

Midway across the bridge is a brass cross (below) where John of Nepomuk's (see p43) body was thrown into the river. It is said that wishes made at the cross will come true.

④ Statue of St John of Nepomuk

At the base of the statue of St John (right) is a brass relief showing a man diving into the river. Rubbing it to attract good luck is an old local tradition; petting the adjacent brass dog is a new one.

⑤ Statue of Sts Cyril and Methodius

Greek missionaries who brought both Christianity and the Glagolitic alphabet to the Czech and Slovak lands, Cyril and Methodius are revered figures in both countries to this day. Karel Dvořák created this statue in 1928–1938 at the peak of Czechoslovakia's National Awakening following independence.

6 Statue of Bruncvik

Peer over the bridge's southern edge to see the Czech answer to King Arthur. Bruncvik **(left)**, a mythical Bohemian knight, is said to have had a magical sword and helped a lion fight a seven-headed dragon. He and his army are promised to awaken and save Prague at the city's most desperate hour.

7 Our Lady of the Mangles

The portrait of Mary hanging on the house south of the bridge is tied to an ancient tale of miraculous healing. Seeing the light go out on the balcony below is supposedly an omen of imminent death – don't stare too long.

8 Statue of St Luitgard

Matthias Braun's 1710 depiction **(right)** of a blind Cistercian nun's celebrated vision, in which Christ appeared to her and permitted her to touch his wounds, has a timeless appeal.

NEED TO KNOW

MAP J4 ■ 775 400052

Malá Strana bridge tower: www.prague.eu/malostranske-mostecke-veze

Old Town bridge tower: www.prague.eu/staromestska-mostecka-vez

Both towers: Opening hours vary, check website; adm

■ The Malá Strana bridge tower houses an exhibit on the history of the bridge. The Old Town bridge tower has an exhibit on Charles IV and the bridge.

9 Malá Strana Bridge Towers

Charles Bridge ends at the stone archway connecting Malá Strana's two bridge towers. The smaller, stockier structure on the left is the Judith Tower, which dates to the 12th century.

WHEN TO VISIT CHARLES BRIDGE

During summer, and increasingly year-round, the bridge is well nigh impassable throughout the day, crowded with artists, tourists and the odd Dixieland jazz band. It is best seen in the early hours as the sun rises over the Old Town bridge tower. A late evening stroll gives a similarly dramatic view, with the illuminated cathedral and castle looming above.

10 Statue of the Trinitarian Order

This religious order was set up to ransom prisoners of war from the Crusades and buy Christians back their freedom, hence the depiction of a bored Turk keeping guard outside a cell **(left)**.

TOP 10 ⭐ Loreta

At the heart of this sparkling 17th-century Baroque pilgrimage site is its claim to fame and most proud possession: a replica of the original Santa Casa in Loreto, Italy, believed to be the house where the Virgin Mary received the Incarnation. Construction of the grandiose church and the surrounding chapels coincided with the Counter-Reformation, and one of Prague's first Baroque buildings was intended to lure Czechs back to the Catholic faith.

1 Loretánské náměstí

This square is said to have been a pagan burial ground. The stucco façade of Loreta (right) is dwarfed by the Černín Palace opposite, home of the Ministry of Foreign Affairs.

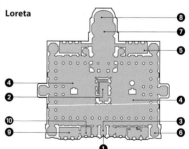

2 Santa Casa

The stucco reliefs on the outside of this replica (above) of the Holy Family's house in Nazareth depict scenes from the life of the Virgin Mary. Inside stands the miracle-working statue of Our Lady of Loreto.

Loreta

3 Bell Tower

The carillon was the gift of a merchant of Prague whose daughter was healed by the intercession of the Lady of Loreto. An automated mechanism chimes a Marian hymn every hour.

4 Inner Courtyard

In this courtyard, visitors can admire two Baroque fountains (right). The south fountain depicts the Assumption of the Virgin; the north features a sculpture of the Resurrection.

Previous pages Sunset over Charles Bridge, with Prague Castle in the background

5 Arcade

Before and after visiting the Santa Casa, pilgrims passed through the arcade and prayed at its chapels dedicated to the Holy Family, the Holy Rood, St Francis Seraphim, St Antony of Padua, St Anne and Our Lady of Sorrows.

6 St Wilgefortis Altar

The Chapel of Our Lady of Sorrows contains the altar of a bearded, crucified woman. Wilgefortis (Starosta in Czech) was said to be a Portuguese maiden who prayed for a masculine appearance in order to preserve her chastity.

SANTA CASA

The Santa Casa was the house in Nazareth in which the archangel Gabriel is believed to have announced to the Virgin Mary that she would conceive the Son of God. In the 13th century, the Greek Angeli family moved the house to Loreto, Italy. As the Marian cult spread, copies of the Italian Loreto started emerging all over Europe – the 17th-century Prague site is believed to be the truest representation of the original structure.

8 Altars of Sts Felicissimus and Marcia

On either side of the altar in the Church of the Nativity are large reliquary displays containing the remains of these two Spanish saints.

9 Treasury

The Communists created this exhibit of sacred items **(right)** to show how the papal church brought peasants to obedience with a "cheap promise of happiness beyond the grave".

7 Church of the Nativity

Originally a small alcove behind the Santa Casa, the church **(left)** was expanded into its present size in 1717. The Rococo organ stands opposite the altar, over a crypt to Loreta benefactors.

NEED TO KNOW

MAP B2 ■ Loretánské náměstí 7
■ 220 516740 ■ www.loreta.cz

Open 10am–5pm daily

Adm (under-6s free, family tickets available); audio guides can be hired

■ At Kapucínská 2 nearby is a memorial to people tortured by secret police in the former Interior Ministry building.

10 Prague Sun

The silver monstrance **(left)** for displaying the host – created in 1699 by Johann Bernard Fischer von Erlach – is gold-plated and studded with 6,222 diamonds. The Virgin looks up at her son, represented by the host in the receptacle.

TOP 10 ⭐ Old Jewish Cemetery

The crumbling Old Jewish Cemetery *(Starý židovský hřbitov)* is a moving memorial to the once considerable Jewish community of Prague. This was one of the few burial sites available to the city's Jews, and graves had to be layered when the plot became full. Estimates put it at about 100,000 graves, with the oldest headstone dating from 1439 and the final burial taking place in 1787. The Old-New Synagogue, built in the 13th century, is situated across the street.

① Avigdor Kara's Grave
The oldest grave is that of this poet and scholar, best known for his documentation of the pogrom of 1389, which he survived.

② Mordechai Maisel's Grave
Mordechai Maisel (1528–1601), the mayor of the Jewish ghetto during the reign of Rudolf II, funded the synagogue *(see p110)* that bears his name.

③ Grave of Rabbi Judah Loew
The grave of Rabbi Judah Loew ben Bezalel *(see p110)*, to whom legend attributes the creation of the Prague Golem *(see p54)*, is located here **(left)**.

④ Gothic Tombstones
The eastern wall has fragments of Gothic tombstones rescued from another graveyard near Vladislavova street in 1866. Further graves at another site were found in the 1990s.

Gravestones, Old Jewish Cemetery

⑤ Klausen Synagogue
Mordechai Maisel also commissioned the building of the Klausen Synagogue *(see p110)* on the cemetery's northern edge **(above)**. It now houses exhibitions *(see p49)* on Jewish festivals and traditions.

⑥ Nephele Mound
Stillborn children, miscarried babies and other infants who died under a year old were buried in the southeast corner of the cemetery.

8 David Gans's Tombstone

Gans's headstone **(left)** is marked with a goose and the Star of David, after his name and his faith. A pupil of Loew, Gans (1541–1613) was the author of a seminal two-volume history of the Jewish people. He was also an accomplished astronomer during the time of Johannes Kepler (see p43).

9 Grave of Rabbi Oppenheim

Rabbi David Oppenheim was the first chief rabbi of Moravia, and later chief rabbi of Bohemia and finally of Prague, where he died in 1736.

10 Zemach Grave

The gravestone of the printer Mordechai Zemach (d 1592) and his son Bezalel (d. 1589) lies next to the Pinkas Synagogue (see p111). Mordechai Zemach was a co-founder of the Prague Burial Society.

NEED TO KNOW

MAP K2 ■ Josefov

Old Jewish Cemetery: Široká; 222 749 211; open Apr–Oct: 9am–6pm Sun–Fri (Nov–Mar: to 4:30pm); closed Jewish holidays; adm (ticket valid for 1 week, includes entrance to various synagogues managed by the Jewish Museum, see p49); audio guides available; www.jewishmuseum.cz

Old-New Synagogue: Červená; open 9am–6pm Sun–Fri (Nov–Mar: to 5pm); adm (under-6s free); www.synagogue.cz

....

■ In the synagogues, it is customary for men to wear a *yarmulka* (skull cap). Look for them at the entrance; return them when you leave.

■ The Museum of Decorative Arts' east windows (see p49) offer excellent views of the cemetery.

---

7 Hendl Bassevi's Grave

This elaborate tombstone **(below)** marks the resting place of the "Jewish Queen", Hendl Bassevi. Her husband, mayor Jacob Bassevi, was raised to the nobility by Ferdinand II and permitted a coat of arms, which can be seen on his wife's gravestone.

Entrance

Old Jewish Cemetery

Old-New Synagogue Features

1 Rabbi Loew's Chair
Topped with a Star of David, the tall chair found by the eastern wall has been reserved for the chief rabbis of Prague throughout the history of the synagogue.

2 Jewish Standard
Prague's Jewish community was permitted a banner in the 15th century as a symbol of its autonomy. The copy hanging above the bimah replicates a 1716 original, featuring a Jewish hat within a six-pointed star and bearing the legend "Shema Yisroel".

The nave of the synagogue

3 Nave
Twelve narrow windows, evoking the 12 tribes of Israel, line the perimeter walls, which are unadorned save for the abbreviation of biblical verses. Two central pillars are modelled on the façade columns of the Temple of Jerusalem.

4 Ark
Behind the curtain on the eastern wall are the Torah scrolls, which are kept in the holy ark. The tympanum features foliage and grape motifs, which are also found in the nearby St Agnes of

The roof and attic of the synagogue

Bohemia Convent (see pp34–5), and date from the synagogue's construction in the late 13th century.

5 Entrance
The biblical inscription "Revere God and observe His commandments! For this applies to all mankind" admonished worshippers as people were entering and leaving the synagogue.

6 Vaulting
To avoid forming the sign of the cross, a fifth rib was added to the nave's vaulting, which is decorated with vine leaves and ivy.

7 Women's Windows
Women were not permitted in the nave of the synagogue, but sat in the vestibule. Narrow openings in the wall allowed them to follow the services being conducted within.

8 Bimah
A pulpit stands on this dais in the centre. From here the rabbi reads the Torah and performs wedding ceremonies.

9 Josefov Town Hall
Adjacent to the synagogue stands the Jewish Town Hall (see p110). The hands of the clock on the façade run anticlockwise – or clockwise if you read Hebrew.

10 Attic
Legend has it that Rabbi Judah Loew stashed the remains of the Golem (see p54) he had created under the synagogue's large saddle roof.

PRAGUE'S JEWISH COMMUNITY

Prague's Jewish community has been integral to the development of the city. Prominent Jewish people, like Rabbi Loew (see p110) and Mordechai Maisel (see p43) paved the way for Jewish participation in the National Revival of the 19th century. In the 20th century, the works of Jewish author Franz Kafka (see p50) reached global fame – today, the Kafka Museum is one of the city's biggest draws. However, since arriving in the city in the 10th century, Prague's Jewish community has been subject to anti-Semitism. Pogroms such as the infamous Passover slaughter of 1389 – in which 3,000 Jewish people, including those who had taken refuge in the Old-New Synagogue, were killed – have devastated the community. Violence has persisted over the centuries, stoked by political upheavals in Europe. Notably, the 1899 trial of Leopold Hilsner (a Jewish man accused of ritual murder) began an anti-Jewish campaign in the city. Tomáš Garrigue Masaryk, future President of Czechoslovakia, was teaching in Prague's Charles University at the time; his support for Hilsner helped sway public opinion to some degree. In 1939 after the Nazis occupied Prague, Hitler took possession of Czech lands and deported the Jewish population to concentration camps – he reportedly planned to create a museum of the Jewish population as an extinct race in Josefov. By the end of the war, nearly 80,000 Jewish people from Bohemia and Moravia had died in the Holocaust; Prague's Jewish population has never fully recovered.

TOP 10
JEWISH LEADERS

1 Eliezer ben Elijah **Ashkenazi** (1512–85)

2 Judah Loew ben **Bezalel** (c 1520–1609)

3 Mordechai Maisel (1528–1601)

4 Mordechai ben **Abraham Jaffe** (1530–1612)

5 Ephraim Solomon **ben Aaron of Luntshits** (1550–1619)

6 Joseph Solomon **Delmedigo** (1591–1655)

7 David ben Abraham **Oppenheim** (1664–1736)

8 Yechezkel ben Yehuda **Landau** (1713–93)

9 Solomon Judah Lieb **Rapoport** (1790–1867)

10 Efraim Karol Sidon (b 1942)

Terezín was a holding camp north of Prague. Jewish people were moved here by the Nazis during World War II. From there, many were later transported to Nazi-run extermination camps in occupied Poland.

Trade Fair Palace

Surrounded by the Art Nouveau tenement buildings of Holešovice, the austere Trade Fair Palace *(Veletržní Palác)* is a daring work of art in itself. It was the first official Functionalist building in Europe, and even Swiss-French architect Le Corbusier was impressed when he visited Prague in 1928. In 1979, plans were launched to turn the former trade fair complex into the home of the National Gallery's modern and contemporary art collection. The space was inaugurated in 1995, with works by prominent Czech artists alongside a rich array of international masters.

1 House in Aix-en-Provence

The National Gallery's impressive collection of French art was begun in 1923, when Czech president Tomáš Masaryk helped found a small collection. This bright work showing a large tan house (c 1887) by Paul Cézanne was one of those original 25 pieces.

2 Bonjour, Monsieur Gauguin

Paul Gauguin originally painted this simple, flat self-portrait **(above)** as a decoration for the lower panel of a dining-room door in an inn in Le Pouldu, Brittany. The much-admired 19th-century French artist painted this enlarged copy in 1889.

3 Green Wheat

Van Gogh's encounter with Impressionism was a decisive moment. Charmed by the southern French countryside, he created bright canvases such as this 1889 landscape **(above)**.

4 Anxiety

Otto Gutfreund paved the way for modern Czech sculpture. This bronze 1912 work captures the apprehension of man in the early 20th century.

5 St John the Baptist

Auguste Rodin's 1878 sculpture is a study of spiral motion and the natural movement is heightened by his visible muscles, from the tension of the firmly anchored feet, to the trunk, to the head turned away from the dominant gesture of the hand **(right)**.

6 Three Dancing Girls

This striking 1925 oil painting was made by Toyen, a non-binary Czech artist and Surrealist who was born Marie Čermínová. The painting depicts three semi-nude female dancers looming over a small group of smartly dressed men.

7 Self-Portrait

One of 14 Picassos donated in 1960 by former National Museum director Vincenc Kramář, the almond-shaped eyes and triangular nose of this 1907 work testify to the influence of Iberian art.

8 Head of a Young Girl

Henri Laurens's 1926 bronze sculpture is a synthesis of Cubism and the classical ideal of form and beauty. It was added to the collections in 1935.

NEED TO KNOW

MAP B5 ■ Dukelských hrdinů 47, Holešovice ■ 224 301122 ■ www.ngprague.cz

Open 10am–6pm Tue–Sun; adm

....

■ The ground floor and mezzanine house the temporary exhibits. The exhibits shown on these pages are part of the regularly changing medium-term exhibitions. Call ahead for further details.

GALLERY HISTORY

Plans for a trade fair complex began in 1924. A design competition selected the work of architects Oldřich Týl and Josef Fuchs. Only the existing Trade Fair Palace was completed; the other planned buildings never materialized due to a lack of funding. The Trade Fair Palace opened in 1928 but was badly damaged by fire in 1974. It was reopened as a gallery in 1995.

9 At the Moulin Rouge

Toulouse-Lautrec thrived on depictions of Paris nightlife such as this oil tempera **(above)** on cardboard. One of the dancing women is his muse, Jane Avril. Oscar Wilde is one of the figures in the background.

Myself, Self Portrait 10

With the city of Paris and the elements of modern civilization in the background, Henri Rousseau's self-portrait with a palette in hand in the foreground, painted in 1890, depicts impressively the artist as a self-assured personality **(right)**.

TOP 10 ⭐ St Agnes of Bohemia Convent

The 13th-century St Agnes of Bohemia Convent (*Klášter sv. nežky Ceské*) is a Gothic building closely tied to Czech statehood. Daughter of Czech King Přemyšl Ottokar I, Princess Agnes chose a spiritual life and founded a convent here in 1234 for the Poor Clares, an order of nuns associated with the Order of St Francis. However, it was Agnes's diplomatic skills and work in establishing the convent which raised Bohemia in the eyes of Rome, as much as any courtly efforts to do the same. Restored in the 1980s, the convent is now part of the National Gallery and exhibits medieval and early Renaissance art.

1 Strakonice Madonna
This larger-than-life, 700-year-old statue of the Virgin and Child is the Czech National Gallery's most prized possession. The gestures of the Madonna are strikingly rigid, and evoke the Classical French sculpture found in places such as Reims Cathedral.

2 Zbraslav Madonna
Bohemia's most celebrated Marian painting is evocative of Byzantine icons in its style. The ring on the Madonna's left-hand finger symbolizes the church through the mystical marriage between Christ and the Virgin Mary. The work was moved to the St Agnes of Bohemia Convent from the Cistercian Zbraslav Monastery where the majority of the Přemyslid kings were laid to rest.

Vyšší Brod Altarpiece 3
The 14th-century cycle begins with the *Annunciation*, then proceeds through the *Adoration of the Magi* to *Pentecost* **(right)**. The creator of these beautiful panels is unknown.

4 Works of Master Theodoricus
Parts of an altar set on loan from Karlštejn Castle, these works include *St Charlemagne*, *St Catherine*, *St Matthew* **(left)**, *St Luke*, *St Ambrose* and *St Gregory*.

ST AGNES OF BOHEMIA

St Agnes of Bohemia was a powerful figure in medieval politics. Gregory IX granted her convent special privileges and his successor Innocent IV sent relics to be housed there. Agnes died in 1282, but her influence on Czech statehood was felt much later when, in 1989, Pope John Paul II canonized her; five days later, the Velvet Revolution (see p43) began.

6 Třeboň Altarpiece

Only three of the five double-sided panels of the 14th-century retable Třebon Altarpiece **(left)** have survived to the present day.

7 Capuchin Cycle

The origin of these 14 panels is unknown. The Virgin Mary is flanked by St Peter on the left and Christ on the right.

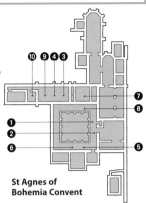

St Agnes of Bohemia Convent

8 Velhartice Altarpiece

Originating in south Bohemia around 1500, this is a rare example of a completely preserved altar **(right)**. Beneath the Madonna, cherubs hold the *vera* icon.

9 Martyrdom of St Florian

Albrecht Altdorfer created this painting **(below)** as part of a multipanel altar featuring scenes from the legend of St Florian. Other pieces from the series are in Florence.

NEED TO KNOW

MAP M1

■ U Milosrdných 17

■ 224 301122

■ www.ngprague.cz

Open 10am–6pm Tue–Sun; adm

Gardens: open 10am–10pm daily (Nov–Mar: to 6pm)

■ Visitors can visit and relax in the two cloister gardens that are complemented with sculptures by leading artists. Entry is free.

5 Puchner Altarpiece

St Agnes gave up a life at court to pursue a spiritual vocation. On this 15th-century altarpiece, she is typically depicted nursing the sick.

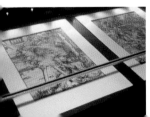

10 Apocalypse Cycle

Although Albrecht Dürer is considered the foremost German Renaissance artist, he is best known to many for his woodcuts, such as this series of 15 **(left)**, which date from 1498 and retain a strong Gothic flavour.

TOP 10 ★ Wenceslas Square

This former medieval horse market began to be redeveloped in the 19th century, rapidly becoming the commercial hub of Prague. In 1848 it was renamed Wenceslas Square *(Václavské náměstí)* in honour of Bohemia's patron saint. The majority of the buildings seen today date from the early 20th century, and their beautiful Art Nouveau façades illustrate how keenly this style was embraced by Czech architects of the time. The square has often been the scene of historic events, most recently in 1989, when large, jubilant crowds gathered here to celebrate the end of Communism.

1 National Museum

Invading Warsaw Pact troops shelled the Neo-Renaissance building in 1968 *(see p118)*, mistaking it for the country's parliament (you can still see the pockmarks). The entry fee is worth it, if only to see the grand marble stairway **(left)** and pantheon of Czech cultural figures.

2 St Wenceslas Statue

The Přemyslid prince sits astride a horse flanked by other Czech patrons **(right)** in Josef Myslbek's 1912 sculpture. The area "under the tail" is a traditional meeting place for locals.

Wenceslas Square

3 Communist Memorial

In front of St Wenceslas is a memorial to the victims of Communism, such as the two men who died protesting against the 1968 invasion.

5 Palác Lucerna

Václav Havel's grandfather designed and built this building, now home to an art gallery, cinema, cafés, shops and a ballroom.

4 Palác Koruna

Built in 1912 in Geometric Modernist style, this "palace" **(right)** held offices, homes and Turkish-style baths. The listed building now hosts the Koruna Palace shopping centre, which has several cafés and luxury stores.

HISTORIC DEMONSTRATIONS

Wenceslas Square saw its first demonstration in 1419 when Catholic reformer Jan Želivský led a procession to St Stephen's Church. On 28 October 1918 the area witnessed Czechoslovak independence. In 1969, student Jan Palach set himself on fire here as a political protest against the Soviet occupation. It is still a scene for political protests.

Grand Hotel Evropa ⑥
Built between 1903 and 1906, this Art Nouveau building **(right)** is an architectural gem. The interior is closed for renovation, but you can still marvel at its beautifully preserved façade.

⑦ Upside-Down Statue
Hanging in the central passage of the Palác Lucerna is David Černý's take *(see p62)* on Czech patron saint Wenceslas.

⑨ Franciscan Garden
A stone's throw from the busy Wenceslas Square, this former monastery garden **(below)** provides much-needed peace *(see p115)* from the city bustle.

⑩ Svobodné slovo Balcony
During the Velvet Revolution *(see p43)*, Václav Havel addressed supporters from the balcony of the *Svobodné slovo* newspaper building. When the deposed Alexander Dubček joined him, the crowds knew that Communism was over.

NEED TO KNOW

MAP N6 ■ New Town
....
■ Cafés, restaurants and shops line both sides of the square from top to bottom.

■ Owing to the high volume of tourists, pickpockets are most active in Wenceslas Square. Be especially wary at the square's northwestern end (around Můstek metro).

⑧ Church of Our Lady of the Snows
Founded by Charles IV upon his coronation in 1347, this beautiful church **(above)** was to have been more than 100 m (330 ft) long, but it was never completed.

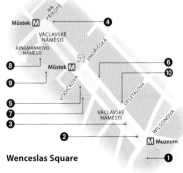

Wenceslas Square

🔟 ⭐ Petřín Hill

Covered with forests and orchards, Petřín Hill is a soft counterpoint to the spires of Hradčany on the Vltava's left bank. Rising more than 300 m (1,000 ft) above sea level, the area began life as a vineyard in the 15th century, but has been a public park since 1825. Early chronicles say it was the site of pagan rituals to the god Perun, and believers still practise ancient rites here on 1 May each year. The park is the perfect place to take a break from the city – stroll along old pathways or take the funicular to see the sights atop the hill.

Observation Tower ①

Modelled after the Eiffel Tower in Paris, Petřín Hill's 63.5-m (210-ft) *Eiffelovka* **(right)** stands only one-quarter as high as its inspiration. The tower was created for the Jubilee Exposition of 1891. A climb of 299 stairs leads to the viewing platform.

② Strahov Stadium

This stadium **(below)** is the largest arena of its kind in the world. Built for Sokol, a physical exercise organization, it was used for gymnastic rallies. Today it is a rock concert venue *(see p46)*.

③ Strahov Monastery

Founded in 1140, Strahov houses the nation's oldest books in the Strahov Library **(below)** while still functioning as a monastery. The Theological Hall, with its frescoes and statue of St John, is a must-see.

NEED TO KNOW

MAP B4 ■ Malá Strana

Funicular: open 8am–11pm daily; adm; www.dpp.cz

Observation Tower: Hours vary, check website; adm, www.prague.eu/petrinska-rozhledna

Mirror Maze: open Apr, May & Sep: 9am–7pm daily (Jun–Aug: to 8pm); Oct–Mar: 10am–6pm daily; adm; www.prague.eu/bludistepetrin

Strahov Monastery: open 9am–noon & 12:30–5pm daily; adm; www.strahovskyklaster.cz

Church of St Lawrence: Closed to public except during Masses (Sun, Mon or Fri)

Štefánik's Observatory: Hours vary, www.planetum.cz; adm

Kinský Summer Palace: open 10am–6pm Tue–Sun; adm; www.nm.cz

■ Nebozízek restaurant (*Petřínské sady 411*) offers spectacular views.

■ There is also a café in the entrance hall of the Observation Tower.

6 Karel Hynek Mácha Statue
Mácha is a national poet, best loved for his Romantic poem "May". On 1 May, admirers lay flowers at his statue.

4 Hunger Wall
The 14th-century wall **(above)** was once part of the city's southern fortifications. Charles IV is said to have ordered its construction as a project to feed the poor during a famine.

7 Church of St Lawrence
This onion-domed church **(below)** was built on a pagan shrine in the 10th century and rebuilt in Baroque style in the 18th century.

8 Štefánik's Observatory
Operating since 1928, the observatory **(below)** was named after M R Štefánik, a Slovak diplomat, scientist and astronomer and the co-founder of the Czechoslovak Republic.

5 Mirror Maze
After laughing at the distorting mirrors in the labyrinth *(see p64)*, take in a bit of history with a diorama depicting the last major military action of the Thirty Years' War on Charles Bridge.

7 Kinský Summer Palace
On the Smíchov side of Petřín Hill, this 19th-century palace (not to be confused with the Kinský Palace in Old Town Square) houses the National Museum's ethnographic collections.

STRAHOV MONASTERY EXHIBITS
Strahov has suffered pillaging armies, fires and totalitarian regimes. Josef II dissolved most local monasteries in 1783, sparing Strahov on the condition that the monks conduct research at their library. Today the majority of the research involves paper preservation. On display are old books, pictures, ornate gospels and miniature Bibles.

10 Funicular
Do as visitors have done since 1890 and take the funicular railway to the top of the hill and walk down. The cable car offers outstanding views of the castle to the north.

The Top 10 of Everything

The Smetana Embankment and the Novotný Bank as seen from the Vltava

🔟 Moments in History

A church mural of St Wenceslas

1 Wenceslas Assassinated

The "Good King" (actually a duke) was the fourth Christian ruler of Czech lands, succeeding his father Vratislav I. Wenceslas I solidified ties with Rome and with German merchants. Murdered by his brother Boleslav the Cruel in 935, he was later canonized.

2 Charles IV Becomes Holy Roman Emperor

Grandson of an emperor and son of a Přemyslid princess, Charles could hardly help rising to the Bohemian throne in 1347 and to the Roman one in 1355. Prague became the seat of imperial power under his reign, as well as an archbishopric and the home of Central Europe's first university.

Statue of Charles IV in Křižovnické náměstí

3 Hussite Wars

After the Church Council at Constance burned Catholic reformer Jan Hus *(see p19)* at the stake in 1415, his followers literally beat their ploughshares into swords and rebelled against both church and crown. The animosity that resulted between Protestant Czechs and German Catholics would continue to rage for centuries.

4 Reign of Rudolf II

The melancholy Rudolf II (1552–1611), who became Holy Roman Emperor in 1576, was not much good as a statesman and was under threat from his ambitious brother, Matthias, but he was a liberal benefactor

Rudolf II

of the arts and sciences. Among Rudolf's achievements were the support of Johannes Kepler's studies of planetary motion. The emperor also promoted religious freedom.

5 Battle of White Mountain

The Protestant nobility and the emperor continued to provoke each other until hostilities broke into open war. Imperial forces devastated the Czechs in the first battle of the Thirty Years' War in 1620. Czech lands were re-Catholicized, but resentment against Vienna and Rome continued to smoulder.

6 Independence

While World War I raged, National Revival leaders such as Tomáš Masaryk turned to the United States for support for an independent Czechoslovakia. As the war drew to a close in 1918, the Czechoslovak Republic was born.

7 World War II
The First Republic had barely stretched its legs when the Munich Agreement of 1938 gave Czech lands to Nazi Germany. Nearly 80,000 Czech Jews and Romany died in the Holocaust (see p31). After the war, the nation exacted revenge by expelling its German citizens.

8 Under the Communists
Prague emerged from World War II unscathed by bombings, but in 1948 witnessed a Communist coup. During the Communist decades that followed resistance was brutally suppressed. A brief thaw came in 1968, with the Prague Spring when economic and social reforms were introduced that did not sit well with Moscow. Soviet tanks swept through Prague, killing scores of protesters.

Tanks in the streets, Prague Spring

9 Velvet Revolution
After 10 days of mass protests in 1989, the Communist government bowed to the population's indignation. Czechs proudly recall that not even a window was broken during the revolt.

10 Prague Today
Despite the election of seasoned left-wing politician Miloš Zeman as president and former Communist secret police agent Andrej Babiš as prime minister in 2013 and 2017 respectively, the 2020s have seen the rise again of the centre right. In 2021, centre-right leader Petr Fiala became prime minister, with Petr Pavel following as president in 2023. Like much of Europe, the country is facing a mild recession, but tourism remains a substantial source of revenue – after all, Prague is one of Europe's most visited cities.

TOP 10 HISTORICAL FIGURES

Stained-glass painting of St Agnes

1 St Agnes (1211–82)
St Agnes, devout sister of Wenceslas I, built a convent for the order of the Poor Clares (the female counterpart of the Franciscans).

2 St John of Nepomuk (1340–93)
Wenceslas IV killed Nepomuk over the election of an abbot and threw his body from Charles Bridge. He was canonized in 1729.

3 Jan Hus (1370–1415)
Philosopher priest Jan Hus preached against church corruption and was burned as a heretic.

4 Mordechai Maisel (1528–1601)
The Jewish mayor (see p28) was one of the richest men in Europe.

5 Tycho Brahe (1546–1601)
Astronomer at Rudolf's court, Brahe suffered a burst bladder when he refused to leave the emperor's side at a banquet.

6 Johannes Kepler (1571–1630)
The German astronomer pioneered studies of planetary motion.

7 Albrecht von Wallenstein (1583–1634)
Leader of the Catholics during the Thirty Years' War, General Wallenstein built a vast palace (see p96) in Prague.

8 Franz Kafka (1883–1924)
Prague's best-known author, Kafka (see p50) was largely unpublished in his lifetime.

9 Milada Horáková (1901–50)
This Czech politician fought for the equal rights of women and families. She was the only woman executed by the Communist regime.

10 Emil Zátopek (1922–2000)
"The Locomotive" won three gold medals for long-distance events at the 1952 Olympic Games.

⬛🔟 Places of Worship

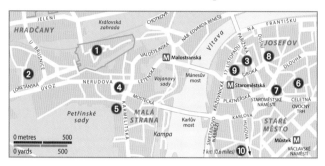

1 St Vitus Cathedral

The current building, looming majestically over the castle complex, is a combination of architectural styles and took almost 600 years to complete. In days of old, the cathedral (see pp16–17) was the setting for spectacular Bohemian coronations conducted by Prague's archbishops. It is also the final resting place of the saints John of Nepomuk and Wenceslas, as well as scores of other notable Czech figures.

Stained glass at St Vitus Cathedral

2 Loreta

At the heart of this elaborate shrine to the Virgin Mary is the Santa Casa – a reproduction of the house where Mary received the Angel Gabriel. Loreta's treasury (see pp26–7) holds several priceless monstrances (open or transparent receptacles) and other artifacts.

3 Old-New Synagogue

Prague's Orthodox Jewish community (see p30) still holds services in this 13th-century synagogue (see p109), which is the oldest in Central Europe. Its curious name may come from the Hebrew Al-Tenai, meaning "with reservation". Legend has it that its stones will eventually have to be returned to Jerusalem, whence they came.

4 St Nicholas Church, Malá Strana

The Malá Strana church clock tower and dome upstage its namesake across the river. The splendid Baroque sanctuary (see p94) was meant to impress Catholic sceptics of the might of Rome.

5 Church of our Lady Victorious

This Baroque church contains the famed statue (see p95) of the Infant Jesus of Prague. The wax baby doll is credited with miraculous powers. The resident Order of English Virgins look after the statue and change his clothes.

6 Basilica of St James

This is an active place of worship. The Baroque façade (see p86) is awash with cherubs and scenes depicting episodes from the lives of saints Francis of Assisi, James and Antony of Padua. There is also a mummified arm hanging above the door inside.

Church of Our Lady before Týn

7 Church of Our Lady before Týn

MAP M3 ■ Staroměstské náměstí 14 ■ Open 10am–1pm & 3–5pm Tue–Sat, 10:30am–noon Sun

The Gothic towers of Týn *(see p18)* loom over Old Town Square's houses. During the Counter-Reformation, the Jesuits melted down the gold Hussite chalice that stood between the towers and recast it as the Madonna seen today.

8 Spanish Synagogue

The present Moorish building with its opulent interior *(see p111)* replaced Prague's oldest synagogue after the latter was razed in 1867. The Conservative Jewish community holds services here. It also houses Jewish Museum exhibits, offices and a reference centre.

9 Pinkas Synagogue

The names of nearly 80,000 Czech victims of the Holocaust *(see p31)* cover the walls of this notable house *(see p111)*, which sits adjacent to the Old Jewish Cemetery,. The women's gallery was added in the 18th century.

Romanesque portal

10 Cathedral of Sts Cyril and Methodius

The assassins of Reinhard Heydrich, the Nazi governor of Czechoslovakia, took refuge in this Eastern Orthodox cathedral *(see p114)* along with members of the Czech Resistance. Surrounded by German troops, they took their own lives on 18 June 1942. The Nazis executed Bishop Gorazd, who had sheltered them. Since 1945, every year on 18 June the cathedral holds a special service to remember the victims of the Heydrich Terror.

The beautiful interior of the Spanish Synagogue

TOP 10 Communist Monuments

The soaring Žižkov TV Tower

1 Žižkov TV Tower

The city's most hated building among Praguers was built between 1985 and 1992, and was intended, so the rumour goes, to jam foreign radio signals or emit nefarious radiation. Its utilitarian design aside, however, the 216-m (709-ft) tower *(see p125)* offers spectacular views of the city skyline on a clear day.

National Memorial on the Vítkov Hill

2 National Memorial on the Vítkov Hill

After a failed attempt to embalm President Klement Gottwald after his death in 1953, the Communist government was forced to cremate their favoured leader. His ashes, as well as those of various other apparatchiks, were buried atop Vítkov Hill, behind the giant 1950 bronze equestrian statue of Jan Žižka, which is one of the world's largest equestrian statues. They were removed after the Velvet Revolution *(see p43)*. Today the monument serves as a museum of Czech and Czechoslovak history *(see p125)*.

3 Strahov Stadium

Prague Castle would fit inside this massive arena situated on Petřín Hill. Built in 1955 for the purposes of *spartakiáda* physical culture performances, this structure was the first concrete panel building in Czechoslovakia. Today, the stadium *(see p38)* has eight football pitches and serves as a training centre for the AC Sparta football team. Some popular bands have also held performances here.

4 Letná Plinth

MAP E1 ■ Letenské sady, Letná

Where sculptor Vratislav Karel Novák's giant metronome now swings there once stood a 14,000-ton statue *(see p124)* of Joseph Stalin – the largest in the world and visible from all over the city – backed by a queue of admiring citizens. Stalin's successor Nikita Khrushchev ordered the statue to be destroyed by a series of dramatic dynamite explosions in 1962. Pop star Michael Jackson launched his 1996 World Tour in Prague, unwisely erecting a statue of himself on the very same spot.

5 Congress Centre

Since its partial reconstruction in 2000, this has become one of the most modern congress centres in Europe. The excellent acoustics in the Congress Hall make it one of the best concert venues in the world, comparable to the famous halls of London, Montreal and Boston. The centre *(see p127)* has capacity for close to 10,000 visitors and is used for a range of events.

6 Anděl Metro Station
MAP B6

In the reconstruction of the Anděl Centre, developers removed an epic mosaic tribute to the friendship between Moscow and Prague, but from the metro platforms below, you can still see frieze tributes to Soviet cosmonauts. Even if you're not riding the metro, you will need a standard ticket to access the platform.

7 Sbratření
MAP H3

■ Vrchlického sady

This 1947 bronze statue by Karel Pokorny recalls the Red Army's liberation of Prague in 1945: a grateful resistance fighter greets a Soviet foot soldier with a bunch of lilac and an embrace. Inspired by a photograph taken in 1945 by Karel Ludwig, this is one of the few pro-Soviet monuments still standing in Prague.

Sbratření or Brotherhood

8 Czech Radio Building
MAP B6 ■ Vinohradská 12, Vinohrady ■ Closed to the public

Warsaw Pact tanks invaded the Czech capital in 1968 to put an end to Alexander Dubček's Prague Spring liberalization. Among those who paid for their resistance with their lives were Czech Radio journalists, who first broadcast the news that the nation was under attack. A plaque in front of the building honours their bravery.

9 Museum of Communism

This museum (see p118) seeks to help visitors experience totalitarianism first hand through reproductions and genuine objects from the Communist era. On display are original artifacts, including photos, propaganda material and film footage. The most chilling is the reconstructed interrogation room.

10 New Building of the National Museum
MAP G5 ■ Vinohradská 1, New Town ■ Open 10am–6pm daily ■ Adm ■ www.nm.cz

From its construction in the 1970s until the country split into the Czech and Slovak republics in 1993, this unnamed building housed Czechoslovakia's Federal Assembly. It was home to Radio Free Europe from 1994 to 2009, and now hosts exhibitions of the National Museum (see p48).

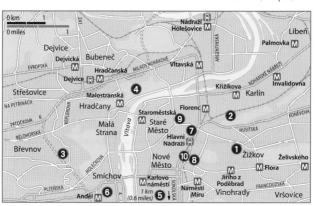

🔟 Museums and Galleries

1 Trade Fair Palace

MAP B2 ■ Dukelských Hrdinů 47 ■ Open 10am–6pm Tue–Sun ■ Adm ■ www.ngprague.cz

The National Gallery's extensive art collection is spread throughout the city in six locations. It opened its museum of 20th and 21st-century art in 1995, and is set in a reconstruction of a Trade Fair building from 1928. Since 2000, it has also hosted a 19th-century collection. Featured in this collection are French artworks, as well as a splendid collection of Czech modern art. Other locations of the National Gallery are the St Agnes of Bohemia Convent (see pp34–5); Sternberg Palace; Schwarzenberg Palace; and the Salm Palace and Kinský Palace (see p19).

National Gallery, Trade Fair Palace

2 National Museum

The country's leading natural history and ethnographic museum (see p118) is housed in a building that dominates Wenceslas Square. The entrance fee is worth it, if only to see the grand marble stairway, the Pantheon and the interior paintings. The annexe across the street holds rotating exhibitions.

3 DOX Centre for Contemporary Art

A multi-functional space located in a former factory, DOX (see p126) showcases unique works of art focusing on current social issues. It also offers special programmes for children.

Interior of the Smetana Museum

4 Smetana Museum

MAP J5 ■ Novotného lávka 1 ■ 222 220082 ■ Open 10am–5pm Wed–Mon ■ Adm ■ www.nm.cz

Part of the National Museum, this grand Renaissance-style building, formerly owned by a water company, is a museum dedicated to the father of Czech music, Bedřich Smetana (see p50). Documents, letters, scores and instruments detailing his life and work are exhibited here.

5 Sternberg Palace

Since 1949, the fine Baroque building of the Sternberg Palace (see p102) has been used to house the Prague National Gallery's collection of European art. The gallery is set over three floors that surround the central courtyard. The collection focuses on the Old Masters, and features renowned artists such as Rembrandt, Rubens, El Greco, Van Dyck, Tintoretto and Goya.

6 The City of Prague Museum

The collection at this museum (see p126) documents the history and cultural development of the Czech capital from prehistory to the 19th century when the Neo-Renaissance building was erected specially for the museum. The exhibition includes china, furniture, relics of medieval guilds, bits of famous Prague buildings and paintings of Prague through the ages. Don't miss Antonín Langweil's remarkable 1:500 scale model of the city, which is made entirely of paper and wood. It is a

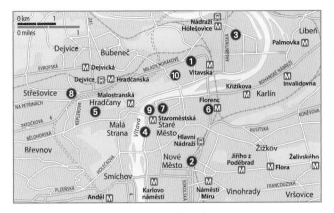

snapshot of how the city looked in 1834. The museum also manages 14 other buildings located around the city that all house exhibitions.

7 Jewish Museum

MAP L3 ■ Ticket centre: Maiselova 38/15 ■ All sites: open 9am–6pm Sun–Fri (winter: to 4:30pm) ■ Adm ■ www.jewishmuseum.cz

This museum's collection of Judaic art is perhaps the world's largest, with 40,000 artifacts and 100,000 books. Other exhibits present the lives and history of the Jewish people in Bohemia and Moravia. The museum consists of the Old Jewish Cemetery (see pp28–9), the Ceremonial Hall (see p110), the Robert Guttman Gallery and four historical synagogues – the Maisel, the Klausen, the Pinkas and the Spanish (see pp110–11). All of the museum sites are covered by a single ticket, which is available from the ticket office, the synagogues (except the Maisel) or online.

8 Public Transport Museum

MAP A1 ■ Patočkova 2 ■ Open 9am–5pm Sat & Sun ■ Adm ■ www.dpp.cz/muzeum-mhd

This museum celebrates more than 100 years of Prague's transport systems. Exhibits range from horse-drawn carriages to the metro, along with unique photographs and models.

9 Museum of Decorative Arts

MAP K3; 17. listopadu 2; 778 543900; open 10am–6pm Wed–Sun (to 8pm Tue); adm ■ House at the Black Madonna: MAP F3; Ovocný trh 19; open 10am–6pm Tue–Sun; www. upm.cz

The museum focuses on historical and contemporary crafts, applied arts and design. Exhibitions on Cubism are held at House at the Black Madonna, a classic Czech Cubist building.

10 National Technical Museum

MAP F1 ■ Kostelní 42 ■ Open 9am–6pm Tue–Sun ■ Adm ■ www.ntm.cz

This is the ultimate how-things-work museum, with exhibitions on everything from mining and metallurgy to transport and astronomy. Ask a guide to show you the coal mine in the basement.

Exhibit, National Technical Museum

TOP 10 Writers and Composers

4 Jaroslav Hašek

A notorious joker and the author of the celebrated satirical dig at the Austrian army, *The Good Soldier Švejk* (published in 1921), Hašek was also the creator of the Party for Moderate Progress Within the Bounds of the Law.

5 Wolfgang Amadeus Mozart

Prague and Vienna continue to duel over the legacy of the musical genius, with the Czechs always claiming that Mozart loved them better. The composer premiered his opera *Don Giovanni* in Prague's Estates Theatre (see p67) and Prague residents mourned his death in 1791. Regular Mozart concerts are held in the city.

Mozart

Franz Kafka was born in Prague

1 Franz Kafka

Although he wrote in German and almost none of his work was published in his lifetime, Franz Kafka *is* Prague. Many of his disturbing novels seem to foresee the Communist years. His work has inspired other Prague artists: look out for the giant rotating Kafka head outside Quadrio shopping centre by David Černý.

2 Božena Němcová

One of the greatest Czech writers of the 19th century, Božena Němcová was a founder of modern Czech prose. She was particularly interested in folklore – her work consists of short stories and more extensive prose against a rural backdrop. She is known for her novella *Babička* (*The Grandmother*), regarded as a classic of Czech literature.

3 Karel Čapek

This Czech writer is best known for his science fiction and psychologically penetrating novels. With his 1920 play *R.U.R. (Rossum's Universal Robots)* he gave the world a word for an automaton, from the Czech word *robota*, meaning "forced labour".

Karel Čapek

6 Bedřich Smetana

The composer wrote his opera *Libuše*, based on the legendary princess, for the reopening of Prague's National Theatre in 1883. Smetana vies with Antonín Dvořák for the title of best-loved Czech composer; the former's ode to beer in *The Bartered Bride* gives him a certain advantage.

7 Antonín Dvořák

The works of Dvořák, such as his *Slavonic Dances*, regularly incorporate folk music. He composed his final *New World Symphony* while he was director of the National Conservatory in New York City.

Antonín Dvořák

A portrait of Bohumil Hrabal

⑧ Bohumil Hrabal

The poetic author used to sit in the Old Town pub U Zlatého tygra (see p74), taking down the stories he heard there. He died falling from his hospital-room window in 1997.

⑨ Václav Havel

The former Czech president was known as a playwright and philosopher before he became a civil rights activist protesting the Warsaw Pact invasion in 1968 (see p43). His absurdist works and his fame helped draw international attention to the struggles of his country.

Václav Havel at an awards ceremony

⑩ Květa Legátová

A writer and novelist, Legátová is known for *Želary*, a collection of short stories that explore the harsh reality of early 20th-century life in a remote fictional Czech village. In 2002, she was awarded the State Prize for Literature and published *Jozova Hanule*, her autobiographical novel.

TOP 10 WORKS OF ART, MUSIC AND LITERATURE

Detail, Alfons Mucha's *Slav Epic*

1 Slav Epic
Art Nouveau master Alfons Mucha celebrates the Czech mythic past in this cycle of 20 large canvases.

2 The Castle
Kafka worked on this novel of social alienation while living in Prague Castle's Golden Lane (see p13).

3 The Good Soldier Švejk
Hašek was so effective in sending up the army and the Austro-Hungarian empire that Czechs still have a hard time taking authority seriously.

4 Home Cook
At the start of the 19th century, M D Rettigová became a pioneer in the field of culinary literature with this book.

5 R.U.R.
Karel Čapek's science-fiction play is a sometimes dark study of labour relations and social structures.

6 The Grandmother
Author Božena Němcová based the narrator in her 1855 novella *Babička* on her own grandmother, from whom she heard many of these stories.

7 Vltava
Smetana's *Má vlast* (My homeland) is a set of six tone or symphonic poems celebrating Bohemia. The second, *Vltava*, follows the eponymous river's course.

8 New World Symphony
With his ninth symphony, composed in 1893, Dvořák incorporated the style of American folk songs.

9 Disturbing the Peace
Havel meditates on Communism and the values underlying Central Europe's pursuit of democracy.

10 The Unbearable Lightness of Being
The novel is Milan Kundera's non-linear tale of love, politics and the betrayals inherent in both.

⟨TOP 10⟩ House Signs

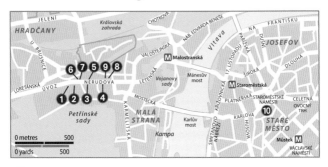

① The White Swan
Nerudova 49

Prague houses weren't given identifying numbers until 1770, when Empress Maria Theresa brought the famed Habsburg trait of orderliness from Vienna to the banks of the Vltava. Before that, homes were known and located by a charming but confusing system of allegorical symbols. Although you can still find such emblematic addresses throughout the older parts of the city, Nerudova street in Malá Strana (see p93) has the highest concentration of house signs in the city. Originally many of them had local significance, although today much of their meaning has been lost. The White Swan is one of these, and probably originated as a golden goose (not to be confused with the downtown department store of the same name, Bílá Labut').

② The Two Suns
Nerudova 47

This house was once the home of the much-loved Czech poet and author Jan Neruda (1834–91), after whom the street is named. Traditionally, this was the writers' and artists' area of Prague, and Neruda conveyed the Bohemian

The Two Suns

atmosphere of Malá Strana in his work. The connection continues today with the quarter's many small art galleries and craft shops.

③ The Golden Key
Nerudova 27

Castle goldsmiths, such as the ones who worked at this house in the 17th century, paid fees to the city, unlike their colleagues who lived in the castle's Golden Lane (see p13). As such, they were entitled to advertise their wares, as preserved today in this building's façade.

④ The Red Lamb
Nerudova 11

One of the street's more unlikely symbols, the scarlet sheep adorning this façade has a significance so arcane, not even the current house owner can explain it. It remains in place as one of the city's many charming idiosyncrasies.

⑤ The Golden Wheel
Nerudova 28

This house symbol may have had something to do with alchemy – the wheel represents a stage in the *magnum opus*, the process by which the base metal lead was purportedly turned into gold.

The Green Lobster
Nerudova 43

Who knows what they were thinking when they hung the crustacean above their door – probably trying to keep up with the neighbours at the Pendant Parsnip (No 39).

7 The Golden Horseshoe
Nerudova 34

The ornate doorway of this beautiful pale-blue building is adorned with an image of St Wenceslas on horseback. Below this dangles a golden horseshoe; it's likely that this was once the home or workshop of a blacksmith.

8 The Devil
Nerudova 4

Lucifer pops up as a cuddly character on houses all over town and in local legend, more a folksy trickster than a sinister prince of darkness.

9 The Three Fiddles
Nerudova 12

They say a demonic trio screeches on their instruments here on moonlit nights. The house was home to a family of violin-makers in the early 18th century, and the sign advertised their trade. Like many of the other buildings on this street, it is now home to a restaurant.

The image of St Wenceslas's Horse

10 St Wenceslas's Horse
Staroměstské náměsti 16

This mural can be seen on the façade of Štorch House (also referred to as "At the Stone Virgin Mary") located at the Old Town Square *(see p18)*. Created by Mikoláš Aleš, it acts as a tribute both to the patron saint of Bohemia and the blacksmiths who shod horses bound for the castle.

Beautifully crafted house sign indicating the Three Fiddles

TOP 10 Haunted Places

The atmospheric interior of Ghosts and Legends Museum

1 Ghosts and Legends Museum

MAP D3 ■ Mostecká 18
■ www.mysteriapragensia.cz

Uncover old Prague's most famous mysteries and legends in this museum exploring the city's ghosts and stories. The atmospheric cellar has a replica of some of old Prague's streets, while the ground floor offers more traditional exhibits that provide background to the legends. All of the material on show is based on original records.

2 Turk in Ungelt

Among the merchants who lived in the Týn settlement behind the Church of Our Lady (see p45) was a Turkish immigrant. When his betrothed ran off and married another, he flew into a rage and chopped her head off. He is said to wander around the Ungelt courtyard carrying the decapitated head.

3 One-Armed Thief

The story of the thief who sought to steal jewels from a statue of the Madonna in the Basilica of St James (see p44), claims that the stony Virgin seized him by the arm and local butchers had to cut him loose. According to some, the thief still haunts the church asking visitors to help him fetch his arm, which hangs from the wall inside.

4 The Golem

It is said that the Prague rabbi Judah Loew (see p110) created a clay automaton to defend the Jews of the Prague ghetto. When the creature ran amok one day, Loew was forced to deactivate him and stash him in the attic (see p30) of the Old-New Synagogue (see p109).

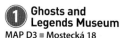

Representation of the Golem

5 The Iron Man

Falsely believing his fiancée to be unfaithful, a knight called off their wedding. After she drowned herself in grief, he realized his mistake and hanged himself. Every 100 years he appears in Platnéřská street to find a young virgin who will free him by talking to him for at least an hour.

6 The Drowned Man

When the bicycle was all the rage in the late 19th century, young Bobeř Říma stole one and rode it into the river. If a soggy young fellow tries to sell you a bike near the Old Town end of Charles Bridge, just keep walking.

7 Emmaus Devil

In an attempt to bedevil the monks at the Emmaus Monastery *(see p117)*, Satan worked there as a cook and laced the monks' food with pepper and other spices. To this day, Czech cuisine has few piquant flavours.

8 Werewolf

Apparently, the gamekeeper of Rudolf II became so enamoured with the wolves that roamed the castle's Stag Moat that he became one himself. Nowadays, he takes the form of a large dog and tends to chase cyclists, joggers and tourists when the whim takes him, so keep looking over your shoulder.

Woodcut (1512) of a werewolf attack

9 Drahomíra

St Wenceslas's mother was, by all accounts, an unpleasant woman. She killed her mother-in-law and might have done in her son, too, but it is said that the gates of hell swallowed her up before she could act. She sometimes wheels through Loretánská náměstí in a fiery carriage.

10 The Mad Barber

When a local barber forsook his home and family after he became caught up in alchemical pursuits, his daughters ended up in a brothel and his wife killed herself. He is said to haunt Karlova and Liliova streets, hoping to return to his honest profession and make amends.

TOP 10 FALSE STORIES

The brass cross on Charles Bridge

1 John of Nepomuk Died on Charles Bridge
Nepomuk was already dead when he was thrown over the side *(see pp22–3)*.

2 Vyšehrad Castle
While it's true that Vyšehrad *(see p123)* was the first seat of power, its importance has been inflated by legend.

3 Alchemists Lived in Golden Lane
Alchemists tended to live on credit in houses in town.

4 Czechs are Believers
In the 2021 census, over 57 per cent of Czechs identified as not having a religion. Over 30 per cent did not declare.

5 Jan Masaryk Committed Suicide
In 1948 the foreign minister was found dead in front of Černín Palace, having "fallen" from a window, according to the Communists.

6 There's Only One Bud
The town of České Budějovice (Budweis in German) was producing beer before the US brewer, but didn't register its copyright on the name.

7 The Danube Flows through Prague
It's incredible how many visitors think the Danube flows through the Czech capital. The river here is the Vltava.

8 Absinth Will Affect Your Mind
The amount of wormwood in the drink is negligible.

9 Czechs and Slovaks are the Same Nation
Despite a shared history and continued affiliation, Czechs and Slovaks have distinct languages, cultures and traditions.

10 Prague is the New Left Bank
After the Velvet Revolution, some proclaimed Prague "the Paris of the 90s", due to the number of expats.

🔟 Eccentric Prague

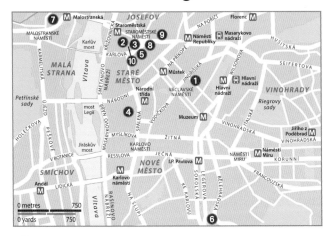

1 Museum of Senses

Challenge your senses at this museum (see p118), where nothing is as it seems. Walk through a jungle in a tunnel where the river flows upwards or stand on top of a skyscraper and step into a desert. The amazing optical illusions here create a fun experience for the entire family.

2 Marionette Don Giovanni

Mozart premiered his opera *Don Giovanni* in 1787 at Prague's Estates Theatre (see p67). Of the two marionette homages to the city's favourite opera, the better production takes place at the National Marionette Theatre (see p67). The technique of the

National Marionette Theatre

puppeteers is so masterful, you'll leave looking for strings attached to passers-by.

3 Pragulic

MAP L4 ■ Staroměstské náměstí 4 ■ 725 314930 ■ www.pragulic.cz

This unusual social enterprise enables you to experience the world from the perspective of homeless people, challenge stereotypes and gain insight into their daily life. Walking tours are organized by guides among the homeless and visitors can choose between short 2-hour tours or a 24-hour one.

4 Prague Golf & Games

MAP E5 ■ Opatovická 18 ■ 723 658293 ■ Open 1–10pm daily (to 11pm Fri & Sat) ■ www.praguegolfandgames.com

The first and only place to offer black light mini golf in the city, Prague Golf & Games is great for people looking for something a little off the beaten track. The interior is almost entirely dark, lit only by neon UV lights. Black light jenga, billiards and pinball are also available. The space can be booked in advance – check the website for more details.

Previous pages Aerial view of the city and St Nicholas Church, Malá Strana

5 Sex Machines Museum
MAP L4 ■ Melantrichova 18 ■ Open 10am–11pm daily ■ Adm ■ www.sexmachinesmuseum.com

An exhibition in a slightly different sense, this is one show that's definitely not for kids. The museum traces the history of instruments for sexual gratification, from their origins to the modern day. While not entirely without cultural merit, the overall package is rather bizarre. There is also, predictably, a gift shop.

6 Folimanka Underground Bunker
Pod Karlovem Street ■ Opening hours vary, check website ■ www.kryt folimanka.cz

This bunker, with an extensive maze of corridors and rooms, was built during the Cold War as a refuge for civilians in case of any nuclear threat. There's also an exhibition with photos of other civilian bunkers located in Prague. This fully functional underground bunker is open to public once a month on a Saturday.

7 Dripstone Wall
MAP D2 ■ Wallenstein Garden, Malá Strana ■ Open Apr–Oct: 7:30am–6pm Mon–Fri (from 10am Sat & Sun; Jun–Sep: to 7pm)

This undeniably eerie wall is on the southeastern edge of the manicured Wallenstein Garden *(see p79)*. From afar, it looks like an enormous wall of grey stalactites but, closer, you'll notice haunting features hidden in the wall, from slithering snakes to grotesque human faces.

8 Museum of Torture
MAP M4 ■ Celetná 12 ■ Open 10am–10pm daily (winter: to 8pm) ■ Adm ■ www.museumtortury.cz

If you can't grasp how these grisly instruments work, the illustrations should make their operation painfully clear. About

Neck trap

100 implements of pain and dozens of etchings are on display, along with explanations in four languages.

9 McGee's Ghost Tours
MAP M3 ■ Týnská 7 ■ 723 306963 ■ www.mcgees ghosttours.com

Whether you are a believer or a sceptic, the guides can guarantee an entertaining evening as they take you through narrow lanes and cobbled alleys to churches and monuments. Learn about alchemists, murderers and the unfortunate souls who lived here. There are four different guided tours that last three hours each.

10 Idiom
MAP K4 ■ Municipal Library of Prague, Mariánské námesti 1 ■ Open 9am–8pm Tue–Fri (from 1pm Mon & Sat)

Located right by the entrance to the Municipal Library of Prague, this eye-catching art installation consists of 8,000 books in a spiral – although, thanks to some clever mirror placement, it appears to go on forever.

Grotto wall at Wallenstein Garden

📖 **Parks and Gardens**

Kampa Island separated from Malá Strana by the Čertovka (Devil's Canal)

1 Petřín Hill
Stroll in the shade of trees and explore all manner of architectural quirks, from a medieval defensive wall to a mini Eiffel Tower, in one of Prague's largest green spaces *(see pp38–9)*. In spring the views are at their best, as the orchards are in bloom.

2 Vyšehrad
Far enough from the centre to be largely tourist-free, Vyšehrad *(see p123)* is the perfect place to be alone with your thoughts. Sights include the Neo-Gothic Sts Peter and Paul Church, the graves of Dvořák and Smetana and reconstructed fortifications. However, visitors should be aware that there's very little shelter from inclement weather.

3 Wallenstein Garden
Albrecht von Wallenstein razed two dozen houses to make way for his expansive "backyard", which features an artificial lake. Among the garden's *(see p79)* stranger elements is the grotto on the south wall, with stalactites imitating a limestone cave. The cries you hear all around you are the resident peacocks.

Wallenstein Garden's Sala Terrena

4 Kampa Island
Malá Strana residents love to sunbathe, sip wine and play frisbee on the island green *(see p94)* of the Little Quarter in summer. However, they also like to smoke marijuana, beat drums well into the night and use the grass for a public dog toilet, so watch your step.

The vibrant Vrtba Garden

5 Vrtba Garden
Arguably the most beautiful in Prague. This Baroque-style garden *(see p95)*, with balustraded terraces, is located right behind Vrtba Palace, on the slopes of Petřín Hill *(see p95)*.

6 Stromovka
King Přemysl Ottokar II established the royal hunting park here in 1266. A public garden since 1804, Stromovka *(see p124)* is one of the city's largest parks. It has four ponds that are ideal for ice-skating

in winter and duck-feeding in summer, and meandering paths that offer easy strolling.

7 Franciscan Garden

Stop here after pounding the pavements of Wenceslas Square and join the pensioners and office workers at lunch, quietly filling the benches behind the Church of Our Lady of the Snows *(see p115)*.

8 South Gardens of Prague Castle

The spectacular views of Malá Strana from these castle-skirting gardens *(see pp12–15)* won't fail to inspire. Enter via the stairs from the Third Courtyard for a pleasant way to conclude a day of sightseeing in Hradčany.

9 Palace Gardens Below Prague Castle

This historic complex of beautiful interconnected terrace gardens is situated on the southern slopes of the Prague Castle in Malá Strana. The gardens abound in rich architectural decoration, decorative staircases, balustrades, scenic terraces, garden-houses and pavilions.

10 Prague Castle Royal Garden

These formal gardens were laid out on the orders of the Habsburg king

Prague Castle Royal Garden

Ferdinand I in 1534 *(see p101)*. After mulling over Queen Anne's summer palace and the Communist-revised frescoes in the Ball Game Hall, slip down to the Stag Moat *(see p102)*.

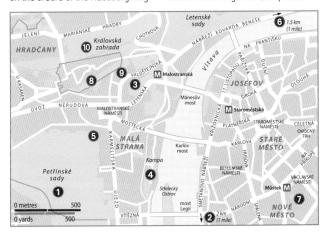

🔟 Off the Beaten Track

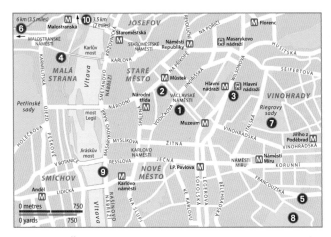

1 David Černý's Upside-Down Horse Statue

MAP N6 ■ Štěpánská 61 ■ 224 225440 ■ Open 8am–midnight daily ■ www. lucerna.cz

Works by Czech installation artist David Černý can be seen around the city, but this hanging statue of St Wenceslas astride an upside-down horse in the central passage of the Palác Lucerna is worth a special look and a laugh. It is a gentle parody of the pompous horse statue at the top of Wenceslas Square.

Upside-Down Horse Statue

2 Cubist Lamppost

MAP M6 ■ Jungmannovo náměstí

The city of Prague was a hotbed of architectural experimentation in the 20th century, enthusiastically embracing the application of Cubist design concepts to all manner of buildings and objects, including – apparently – lampposts. The only one of its kind in the world, this street light can be found on a corner between Václavské náměstí and Jungmannovo náměstí.

Cubist Lamppost

3 Fantova Kavárna

MAP H4 ■ Wilsonova 80 ■ 601 006680 ■ www.fantova-kavarna.cz

The old part of Prague's main train station, Hlavní nádraží, is a beautiful building. Head upstairs from the grand concourse to admire the opulent 1909 Art Nouveau Fantova Kavárna, named after the station's architect. The ambience and the beautiful interiors of the renovated station can be appreciated while sipping coffee at the café.

Karel Zeman Museum

④ Karel Zeman Museum
MAP D3 ■ Saský dvůr, Malá Strana ■ 724 341091 ■ Open 10am–7pm daily ■ www.muzeum karlazemana.cz

This hands-on, interactive museum focuses on the work of renowned Czech film-maker Karel Zeman, who directed several noteworthy Czech fantasy films, including *The Fabulous World of Jules Verne* and *The Fabulous Baron Munchausen*.

⑤ Krymská
MAP C6

Prague's nascent hipster scene is thriving along this pleasantly dilapidated street in the district of Vršovice. There are several good cafés and bars, where modern trends and old Prague clash to fascinating effect.

⑥ Divoká Šárka
MAP A5

This expansive nature reserve offers a touch of wilderness within a short tram ride of the centre. There are rugged rock formations, deep forests and even a refreshing stream-fed swimming pool during the summer months. The hilly meadows are a great spot for kite-flying in autumn.

⑦ Riegrovy Sady
MAP H5

This sprawling park, partly designed in the style of an English garden, offers plenty of room to spread a blanket and admire views out over the Old Town with Prague Castle in the distance.

⑧ Grebovka
MAP B6 ■ Havlíčkovy sady 2188 ■ Open 10am–10pm daily ■ www.pavilongrebovka.cz

Vinohrady was once covered by vineyards (that's what the name means). This pleasant gazebo in a park south of Náměstí Míru is all that's left, but it is still a wonderful place to spend a sunny afternoon sipping wine in the open air.

⑨ Náplavka
MAP E6 ■ New Town

The Vltava's eastern bank south of the National Theatre has come into its own as the go-to summer venue, and offers visitors everything from music festivals to farmers' markets.

⑩ Hotel International
MAP B5 ■ Koulova 15 ■ www.internationalprague.cz

Despite spending 40 years under Communism, central Prague has little architecture to show for it. This impressive Socialist-Realist palace – a 1950s gift from the Soviet Union – is a reminder. Check out the period-piece lobby decor.

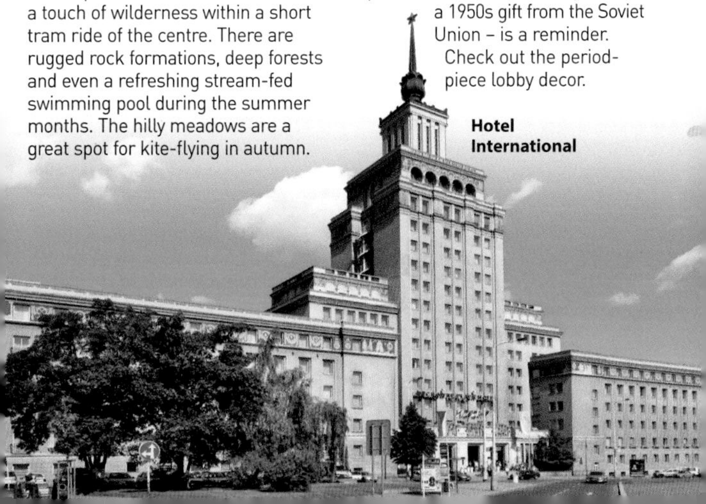

Hotel International

🔟 Children's Attractions

Castle-like entrance of the Petřín Hill Mirror Maze

1 Mirror Maze
The warped mirrors here are great fun for making faces, pointing fingers at elongated bodies and giggling hysterically. For older children interested in a bit of gore and history combined, the battle-scene diorama is another of the many attractions on Petřín Hill (see pp38–9).

2 Swan Feeding
MAP D4
Grab a bag of seeds and head to the riverbank. Střelecký ostrov (island) is an ideal spot to watch graceful white swans dip their necks in the water to catch the morsels, much to children's delight. Take care that kids don't go into the water and mud, however, and make sure that fingers don't get snapped in the feeding frenzy. This is a good activity for all seasons.

3 Puppet Shows
Puppetry is a long-standing Czech tradition, and late afternoon shows will keep your children entertained for up to an hour. There's enough action that younger folk

Czech puppet

usually don't mind not understanding the libretto or narration. Weekend presentations of well-known fairy tales at the National Marionette Theatre (see p67) can fill up quickly, so book in advance.

4 Gargoyle-Spotting
Give the little ones their first taste finding faces on St Vitus Cathedral (see pp16–17) and they'll have their heads pointed upwards for days. In addition to gargoyles, train your kids to spot the innumerable statues, house signs (see pp52–3) and strange faces that adorn arches, cornices and gateways all over the city. Just take care that they don't get stiff necks or stumble on uneven pavement surfaces.

5 National Technical Museum
Located in a huge hanger-like hall, this excellent, hands-on museum (see p49) is sure to be a hit with kids. Inside there are vintage cars and steam trains to clamber on, a mock coal mine and a working TV studio.

6 The Kingdom of Railways

MAP B6 ■ Stroupežnického 23, Smíchov ■ Open 9am–7pm daily ■ www.railroad-kingdom.com

The miniature world of the Railway Kingdom has dozens of model trains and cars, hundreds of metres of track, replicas of important buildings in the Czech Republic, plus an exhibition which features a unique interactive model of Prague at a 1:1000 scale.

7 Výstaviště

Of the few attractions that are open in the Výstaviště exhibition grounds (see p124) is the Czech Republic's largest aquarium, Mořský Svět. In addition to housing hundreds of species of fish, the aquarium has a 100,000-litre tank housing sharks and corals of all kinds. There's also a tank inspired by the legend of Atlantis.

8 Black Light Theatre

MAP K4 ■ Divadlo Ta Fantastika: Karlova 8

There are many black-light shows at theatres (see p66) around the Old Town, but the best one is at Divadlo Ta Fantastika. The brilliant displays should keep youngsters mesmerized.

9 Boat Trips

While adults might enjoy the old-fashioned rowing boats, children will prefer the splashing, pedalling action of the miniature paddleboats on the Vltava. Numerous vendors rent boats and sell tickets near the National Theatre (see p66). Take all the usual precautions to ensure that no one goes overboard.

10 Prague Zoo

Located on a rocky slope north of the centre overlooking the Vltava, the Prague Zoo (see p123) was founded in 1924. It is home to more than 5,000 animals representing close to 700 species, 50 of which are extremely rare in the wild. There are 12 pavilions, including Hippo House, Bird Outlands, Elephant Valley and a Children's Zoo.

TOP 10 SPECIALITY STORES FOR KIDS

1 Michael Puppets
Jilská 22
An assortment of traditional Czech puppets are on offer at this chain.

2 SPARKYS dům hraček Juliš
Václavské náměstí 22
This multi-level store has an excellent selection of toys, games and gifts.

3 Loutky
Nerudova 51
Everything from hand puppets to antique puppets can be found here.

4 Agátin svět
Sokolovská 67, Karlín
Agatha's World offers a range of educational toys for kids of all ages.

5 Hugo chodí bos
Milady Horákové 26, Holešovice
This shop has a lot to offer, from classic Czech toys to educational games.

6 Lego Museum
Národní 362
More megastore than museum, this city centre attraction (see p118) has toys galore.

7 Dřevěný svět hraček
Francouzská 140, Vršovice
At the World of Wooden Toys children can choose from an endless list of items.

8 Space 4 Kids
Milady Horákové 105, Hradčany
This shop is known for its kids furniture sourced from around the world.

9 Truhlář Marionettes
U Lužického semináře 5
Have a puppet custom-made from a photograph at this exciting store.

10 Hamleys
Na Příkopě 14
Known around the world for its range of toys, this branch of Hamleys has a huge carousel inside.

Hamleys toy store in Prague

🔟 Performing Arts Venues

1 State Opera

Set at the top of Wenceslas Square next to the National Museum is the Státní opera *(see p116)*. Originally known as the New German Theatre, it was built to rival the National Theatre. It offers a repertoire heavy on Italian and Viennese favourites.

Graceful exterior of the State opera

2 Divadlo Archa

MAP P3 ■ Na Poříčí 26
■ www.divadloarcha.cz

The premiere venue for avant-garde theatre in Prague, Divadlo Archa has hosted artists such as David Byrne and Compagnie Pál Frenák.

3 Hybernia

MAP P4 ■ Náměstí Republiky 4
■ www.hybernia.eu

Housed in a former monastery, this musical theatre opened in 2006 with the musical *Golem*. It hosts a range of cultural events.

4 Ponec

MAP C6 ■ Husitská 24a, Žižkov
■ www.divadloponec.cz

This contemporary dance and movement theatre space, opened in 2001, has all aspects covered, from top international dance acts to workshops for young talent.

5 Smetana Hall

MAP P3 ■ Náměstí Republiky 5
■ 222 002336 ■ www.fok.cz

The glorious Art Nouveau Smetana Hall at the Municipal House is home to the Prague Symphony Orchestra (Fok). Prague Spring Music Festival *(see p80)* traditionally opens here with Smetana's *Má vlast (see p51)*.

6 National Theatre

The Národní divadlo curtain first went up for Smetana's *Libuše* in 1883; you can still see this or other Czech operas on the same stage. Go to a performance to appreciate the artistic work that went into creating the theatre *(see p116)*.

7 The New Stage

MAP K6 ■ Národní třída 4
■ www.narodni-divadlo.cz

A variety of themes involving dance, music, pantomime, black light and multimedia projections are used by the actors of Laterna Magika to bring alive stories on the stage.

Performance by the artists of Laterna Magika at the New Stage

The 18th-century Estates Theatre

8 Estates Theatre
MAP M4 ■ Ovocný trh 1
■ www.narodni-divadlo.cz

Stavovské divadlo is well known as the venue where Mozart's *Don Giovanni* saw its first performance. It was also the first Czech-language playhouse in what was then a largely German-speaking city. The productions occasionally leave something to be desired, but if you don't see the *Don* here, then where?

9 Rudolfinum
MAP K2 ■ Alšovo nábřeží 12
■ www.rudolfinum.cz

The Rudolfinum is home to the Czech Philharmonic Orchestra. Between 1918 and 1939, and for a brief period after World War II, the Rudolfinum was the seat of the Czechoslovak Parliament.

10 National Marionette Theatre
MAP L3 ■ Žatecká 1

The National Theatre's puppet stage represents the pinnacle of this much-loved genre, staging wonderful productions of Czech fairy tales and other child-pleasing shows (in Czech). They have the best Beatles tribute in town and a marionette version of *Don Giovanni* (see p58).

TOP 10 CHURCHES FOR MUSIC RECITALS

1 St Cajetan Church
MAP C2 ■ Nerudova 22
This magnificent church regularly holds concerts of Bach, Mozart or Brahms.

2 St Agnes of Bohemia Convent
This medieval convent (see pp34–5) regularly holds recitals.

3 St Nicholas Church, Malá Strana
Appreciate the Malá Strana church's Baroque grandeur (see p94) at a concert of sacred music.

4 Basilica of St James
This active house of worship (see p86) regularly invites the general public to hear its organ.

5 Mirror Chapel
The Baroque chamber of the Clementinum (see p86) hosts string quartets and other small ensembles.

6 St Martin in the Wall
MAP L6 ■ Martinská 8
Organ and other recitals are on the bill at this Gothic church, which was once part of the Old Town defences.

7 Spanish Synagogue
The ornate 1880 organ figures in the classic music concerts held in this opulent synagogue (see p111).

8 St George's Basilica
The choral and string recitals here (see p12) present the greatest works of Mozart, Beethoven and others.

9 Church of Sts Simon and Jude
MAP L1 ■ U Milosrdných
Catch an ensemble of the Prague Symphony Orchestra players in this Renaissance sanctuary.

10 St Nicholas Cathedral, Old Town
The Old Town church (see p87) hosts chamber music recitals twice daily.

St Nicholas Cathedral, Old Town

⏏🔟 Clubs

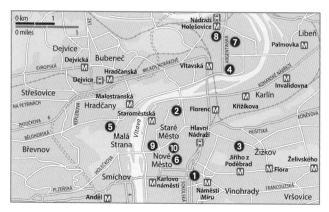

1 Radost FX

The most chic disco in Prague pushes the limits with parties so hedonistic you wonder if there isn't a law against them. Hip-hop, funk and disco are the prevalent flavours on the dance floor (see p119). The vegetarian restaurant serves meals until 11pm. During peak lunch and dinner hours, it can be hard to find a seat.

2 Roxy

The Old Town's most exciting club (see p89), this former cinema is a must for fans of jungle and dub. Parties continue well into the morning, much to the dismay of the neighbours. Such live acts as the Asian Dub Foundation take the stage when it's not occupied by DJs or an experimental theatre production. A portion of Roxy's proceeds goes towards funding Prague's Linhart Foundation, a non-profit organization that promotes contemporary art.

3 Palác Akropolis

In addition to being at the heart of Prague's indie and world-music scene, the Palác Akropolis (see p128) hosts the likes of Ani Difranco, Apollo 440 and Transglobal Underground. The small, smoky Divadelní bar is the hippest, hosting Prague's best DJs. On the ground-floor level is a café and Czech restaurant. On a more cultural note, this is also the best venue in town to hear contemporary Romany music from such local acts as Alom or Věra Bílá and Kale. It is a unique space for music, theatre and art projects.

4 SaSaZu

One of the largest entertainment spaces in Prague, capable of accommodating up to 2,500 guests, SaSaZu (see p128) has welcomed many well-known performers, including British singer Lily Allen, Dutch DJ Tiësto, American rapper Pitbull and pop band One Republic. The hip restaurant offers excellent food from East Asia and has won multiple awards.

The DJ booth and interiors of Roxy

Live music at U Malého Glena

5 U Malého Glena

The shoebox-sized cellar at "Little Glenn's" has to be Prague's smallest jazz venue. The music ranges from African-inspired drumming to blues to modern jazz, and most of it is of a high standard. Upstairs is a restaurant (see p98) where you can get reasonable food and brunch at weekends. Since the venue is tiny, it is advisable to book in advance, especially at weekends.

6 Rocky O'Reilly's

Located in the centre of the city, Rocky O'Reilly's (see p119) is popular with locals, expats and tourists alike. During the day you can settle in to enjoy beer along with fish'n'chips and Irish snacks, or watch your favourite sport on one of many screens. The party starts in the evening with live music performances, often followed by karaoke.

7 Mecca

The proprietors of Mecca (see p128) have turned this former factory in the Holešovice warehouse district into a giant dance-and-dining emporium. The crowd is trendy and the parties cool. A little off the beaten track – take a taxi – but worth it. Visitors can enjoy at the five bars, two stages and three floors of enter-tainment. Opening hours vary, check website before visiting.

8 Cross Club
Plynární 1096, Holešovice
■ www.crossclub.cz

Open from midnight until at least 4:30am every night of the week, this industrial-style club hosts thumping live DJ sets beneath pulsating strobe lights. The dance floors are set among a mass of scrap metal fixtures and steam-punk artwork. The music is usually techno or electronic.

9 Rock Café

Prague's music scene is teeming with so-called "revival bands", most of whom take the stage here with tributes to everyone from Jimi Hendrix to Sadé. There are also several bars and a café. The Rock Café (see p119) has two halls, one of which is primarily reserved for film screenings and theatre and the main music hall has been designed for various music productions.

10 Lucerna Music Bar

Local "big-beat" acts are the mainstay at this music bar (see p119), but it occasionally hosts big names in jazz such as Maceo Parker, as well as where-are-they-now relics (an adjoining venue, the Velký sál, or large hall, hosts bigger acts such as Wynton Marsalis). The club's 1980s and 1990s night is one of the biggest dance parties in town.

Dance floor of the Lucerna Music Bar

🔟 Prague Dishes

Czech guláš with bread knedlíky

1 Guláš
Not as spicy as its Hungarian cousin, Czech goulash is a rich beef stew minus the vegetables. It's always served with *knedlíky* (dumplings), usually made from a mix of bread and potato. Beef forms part of the standard recipe for this staple dish, but you can sometimes find goulash using venison, pork and even vegetarian variants.

2 Řízek
The traditional Czech take on schnitzel is a flattened pork cutlet, covered in flour, egg and breadcrumbs, then fried and served with potato salad. Many pubs offer a chicken or veal alternative, with chips on the side.

3 Nakládaný hermelín
Creamy with an edible rind, this soft cheese is marinated in oil with some pepper, garlic and spices. The main component of this is *hermelín*, the Czech Camembert. A popular bar snack, this is best enjoyed with dark Czech bread and a cold beer.

4 Svíčková na smetaně
This is goulash's sweet cousin: slices of pot-roasted beef tenderloin are served in a carrot-sweetened cream sauce, topped with a dollop of whipped cream and cranberries. Apparently, this was one of President Václav Havel's favourite dishes. Like goulash, it's unthinkable to eat it without the *knedlíky* to mop up the sauce.

A dish of ovocné knedlíky dumplings

5 Knedlíky
These doughy dumplings are the side dish of choice for many gravy-laden Czech dishes. In addition to the savoury varieties, made with bread, potato or bacon *(špekové)*, *knedlíky* also come stuffed with fruit *(ovocné knedlíky)*, the most popular variety being plums *(švestkové)*.

6 Utopence
These pickled sausages, slightly sour, fatty and always piled high with pickled onions,

Nakládaný hermelín with bread

are an ideal accompaniment to the local beer, as a lunchtime or early evening snack.

7 Smažený sýr

Like fried mozzarella sticks, this battered block of deep-fried mild cheese is usually served with French fries (*hranolky*) and a tartar sauce. As with much of Czech cuisine, try not to think about the cholesterol.

8 Vepřoknedlozelo

Vepřové, knedlíky a zelí – pork, dumplings and sauerkraut – are heavy on fat but big on flavour like true Czech soul food. Order it instead of goulash and impress your waiter with how acclimatized you are, assuming you pronounce it right, of course.

9 Halušky

The Germans call these plump little noodles *Spaetzle*. They are included in the Czech culinary canon as a nod to nearby Slovakia, from where they originate. You can order them *s zelím* (with sauerkraut) or *s bryndzou* (with a creamy, sharp cheese). The dish is a filling and cheap Eastern European alternative to pasta.

Traditional dish of *Halušky*

10 Rohlíky

The workhorse of the Prague diet, these ubiquitous banana-shaped bread rolls are served up to accompany the main meal at breakfast, lunch and dinner. Dip them in soft cheese or your dish's sauce, spread them with pâté or order them with a hot-dog on nearly every street corner.

TOP 10 CZECH BEERS

Staropramen beer

1 Staropramen
The hometown favourite has a light, fruity flavour. Brewed in the Smíchov district, its popularity owes as much to marketing as it does to local pride.

2 Pilsner Urquell
The best-known Czech beer on the international market comes from the town of Plzeň, 80 km (50 miles) southwest of Prague. It has a strong, hoppy flavour.

3 Krušovice
Rudolf II established the Krušovice brewery, which produces this sweet and somewhat flat beer. Try the syrupy dark (*tmavé*) variety.

4 Budvar
Brewed in the town of České Budějovice (*see p55*), the beer is no relation to the American Budweiser.

5 Velkopopovický Kozel
This strong, smooth beer is well worth seeking out – some consider it the world's finest.

6 Bakalář
Countryside lager brewed in Rakovník, 50 km (30 miles) west of Prague.

7 Gambrinus
Brewed by Pilsner Urquell, this is the best-selling beer in the country. Try the 11° variety.

8 Bernard
This unpasteurized beer has a distinct, bittersweet flavour and a hoppy aroma.

9 Únětické
This popular microbrew from a small family-run brewery can be hard to find but worth the effort.

10 Svijany
The brewery produces highly rated dark and light beers, including the popular Svijanský Máz pale lager.

🔟 Restaurants

① Kampa Park

Consistently rated Prague's best restaurant, chic Kampa Park *(see p99)* has an unparalleled riverside location in the shadow of Charles Bridge *(see pp22–3)*. The outstanding menu here features influences from all over the world, along with wines from different countries.

La Degustation Bohême Bourgeoise

② La Degustation Bohême Bourgeoise

Among Prague's most wonderful dining experiences, this restaurant *(see p113)* serves a seven-course seasonal tasting menu every evening, as well as a (slightly more affordable) three-course lunch menu. Look out for their delicious takes on classic Czech pork, duck and trout dishes.

③ V Zátiší

Prague was introduced to fine dining at this small Bethlehem Square restaurant *(see p91)*. The *dégustation* menu – a selection of tasters – brings out the kitchen's best and pairs it with select Moravian wines. The Czech specialities and Indian dishes are enhanced by the cosy atmosphere. The seafood is so good you'll forget you're in a landlocked country.

④ La Finestra in Cucina

Traditional and delicious Italian cuisine is served in a cosy setting at this restaurant *(see p113)*. The open kitchen allows diners to watch the chef as he prepares their meal, and an impressive selection of French wines is on offer.

⑤ Terasa U Zlaté studně

Dining atop the hotel of the same name *(see p140)*, guests of "At the Golden Well" *(see p99)* can enjoy the breathtaking views from the beautiful terrace or directly access the Royal Gardens of the Prague Castle during the summer months. The classic Continental cuisine matches the view – but only just. The dining room is tiny, so make sure you make your reservations well in advance.

⑥ Na Kopci

A little way out of the center but worth the trip, this excellent hillside restaurant *(see p129)* serves

The luxurious and modern interiors of V Zátiší

quality Czech cuisine in a relaxed setting. The menu changes with the seasons, but you can usually find locally sourced game like wild boar, deer and rabbit, along with river fish like trout and pikeperch. There are delicious vegetarian options, too.

⑦ Augustine Restaurant

Housed in the beautiful courtyard of a former Augustinian monastery, the Augustine Restaurant *(see p99)* offers a unique culinary experience. The sophisticated European menu, including delicious Czech specialities, is carefully curated by chef Marek Fichtner and his team. A selection of prime wines is also on offer. The setting is a combination of 700 years of history and modern design that inspires the menu and also complements their impeccable service.

⑧ Plzeňská restaurace Obecní dům

It may be a bit touristy, but it's fun nevertheless. Gorgeous tiled mosaics of bucolic Bohemians cover the walls at this restaurant *(see p91)*, while an accordionist rolls out the Beer-Barrel Polka in the evenings. Traditional Czech food and excellent beer are on offer here.

A dish of quail served at Field

⑨ Field

Prague's best example of farm-to-table dining *(see p113)*, with an emphasis on free-range poultry and livestock, local ingredients and simple presentation. The main courses are built around unusual but traditional bases such as smoked beef tongue and rabbit. Reservations are a must.

⑩ Ichnusa Botega Bistro

The owner has brought a piece of his native Sardinia to Prague, so expect big appetizer plates of thinly sliced dried ham, prosciutto and cheeses, followed by mains of fresh fish, pork and pasta at this bistro *(see p99)*. Highlights on the menu include prawns with tomato, red pepper and garlic, and the grilled tuna is especially popular. The wines are homemade and also brought in from Sardinia. Reservations advised.

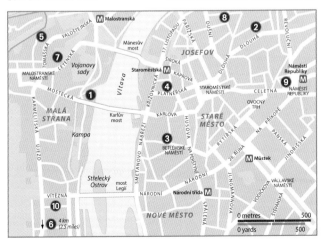

🔟 Bars and Kavárnas

Knights' Hall at U Fleků

1 U Fleků

The city's oldest brewing pub, dating to 1499, U Fleků (see p120) is famous for its delicious dark lager and somewhat more than modest prices. Despite what anyone might tell you, the Becherovka shots are not complimentary and the rounds will keep coming until you say "ne" five times. Very popular with tourists, and not without reason.

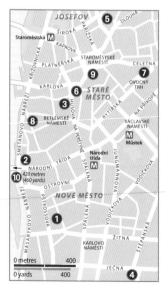

2 Café Slavia

Across from the National Theatre and on a busy river thoroughfare, Café Slavia (see p90) with its 1930s Art Deco interior is a famous literary café. Theatre-goers, actors and playwrights frequent this café. Enjoy a coffee and dessert at the end of the day or after a night at the theatre, admiring the view of the riverside, Charles Bridge and Prague Castle.

3 U Zlatého tygra

This legendary pub (see p90), famed as the haunt of the late writer Bohumíl Hrabal (see p51), serves the finest mug of Pilsner Urquell in Prague. Apart from the Pilsner beer, the brief menu features the famous beer cheese, snacks and coffee. Regulars were indifferent when Václav Havel brought Bill Clinton in for a cold glass when they were both serving presidents, so don't expect them to take much interest in you.

4 Pivovarský dům

Excellent, rustic Czech fare. The house brewmaster is always concocting new flavours for his drinks, such as coffee lager or champagne ale. This is a good place (see p120) to visit if you prefer herbal or fruity flavoured beers such as cherry, nettle and coffee. You can also see the fermenting vats slowly making beer, if the process of brewing interests you.

The cosy Pivovarský dům

5 Kenton's

This is one of Prague's best cocktail bars. It may look like a Jazz Age time capsule, but Kenton's *(see p89)* is actually a relative newcomer, and highly welcome at that. You'll find no bottle juggling, just serious mixology, very dry martinis and, if you're lucky, a seat. Open until 3am. You can also learn a few bartender's tricks at the regular mixology classes.

6 U Tří Růží

This good Czech restaurant and microbrewery *(see p90)* feels just right for the middle of Old Town. The decor includes murals depicting history of brewing in Czech lands. Beers brewed on the premises include a standard light, a dark lager, a Vienna red – from caramelized malt – and a wheat beer. The downstairs area can be crowded and noisy. Reservations are advised.

Grand Café Orient's interior

7 Grand Café Orient

Located on the first floor of the famous House of the Black Madonna, this café *(see p90)* was designed using the Cubist movement in 1912 by Josef Gočár. Patrons will love the building's architecture and be fascinated by the tower of cakes that greets them at the entrance. Grand Café Orient serves tea, breakfast and lunch menus, as well as wine and cocktails.

The elegant decor at Hemingway Bar

8 Hemingway Bar

This is an old-fashioned cocktail bar *(see p89)* exactly as it should be, with formally dressed barmen polishing up the glassware before they pour you the perfect Old Fashioned or Whiskey Sour. The cocktail menu has hundreds of classic mixes, and even a selection of premium Czech, French and Swiss absinth. Book ahead or you're likely to be turned away.

9 Black Angel's

This bar *(see p89)*, located in the second basement of hotel U Prince, features 1930s-style decor among original Gothic and Romanesque stonemasonry. Sip on the excellent cocktails in the sophisticated interior, while enjoying fabulous views of the Old Town Square and City Centre.

10 Café Savoy

With its Art Nouveau interiors and Neo-Renaissance style high ceiling, Café Savoy *(see p99)*, is considered as one of the most gorgeous and stylish cafés in Prague. Set near the Kampa park and Petřín hill, just a few steps from the Vltava river, this café provides the perfect setting to enjoy breakfast or lunch in a grand style. The regularly changing seasonal menu includes a variety of salads, roast meats and Czech specialities. Enjoy your coffee with one of their classic Czech desserts.

⏁⏁10 Shops and Markets

1 Botanicus
Here *(see p88)* you'll find oils and salts for that hot bath your travel-weary feet crave, as well as perfumes, candles, soaps and every natural health and beauty product you can imagine. There are two branches right next to each other just off the Old Town Square.

2 Artěl
Named after a group of Bohemian artisans established in the early 1900s, Artěl *(see p97)* has taken the time-honoured art of glassmaking and, working hand in hand with highly skilled craftspeople, has created a collection of fresh, whimsical yet elegant designs. They have created custom designs for several top luxury brands including Burberry and Gucci.

Decanters, Erpet Bohemia Crystal

3 Erpet Bohemia Crystal
Set in the famous Old Town Square, this is a one-stop shop for glass and jewellery. Erpet *(see p88)* sells Bohemian lead crystal, garnet jewellery, enamel glass and chandeliers, as well as fine goods from the Moser, Goebel and Swarovski manufacturers. Shoppers can ponder the purchases they're about to make over coffee in the shop's comfortable lounge area.

4 Art Deco
Enter this shop *(see p88)* filled with antique furnishings, vintage clothing and one-of-a-kind knick-knacks and you'll feel you've stepped back into the First Republic. Kit yourself out in Jazz Age style, right down to the spats and cigarette holder, or dress up your parlour with an Art Nouveau clock or cordial set.

The chic interiors of Artěl

5 Dorotheum
MAP M4
■ Ovocný trh 2
Dorotheum offices throughout the world trace their roots back to the Vienna pawnbroking office, established by Emperor Josef I in 1707. As a registered member of the Association of International Auctioneers, Dorotheum holds large auctions several times a year and maintains a huge sales gallery of paintings and works of art, jewellery, silverware, glassware, fine china and furniture, as

well as other collectors' items. Their regular auctions are popular with local as well as foreign clients.

⑥ Manufaktura

This popular gift shop chain *(see p88)*, an original Czech brand, is known for offering a unique range of natural cosmetic products and accessories as well as selling traditional Czech and Moravian souvenirs. Manufaktura's line of cosmetics, made with natural ingredients, and the attractive accessories including scented candles, porcelain and massage tools are ideal for home spa.

Cosmetics on display at Manufaktura

⑦ Local Artists Praha
MAP L4 ▪ Karlova 21

While walking through the "souvenir" Karlova street, set aside the time to stop at this small shop, where every item on display is a testimony to Czech traditional arts and crafts. The unique collection includes hand-made pottery and beer cosmetics.

⑧ Hračky U zlatého lva

This centrally-located, multi-storey toyshop *(see p88)* stocks a huge selection of traditional Czech wooden toys, most of them locally produced. There's a Krtek (Little Mole – the most popular Czech cartoon character) theme throughout which will please travelling tots in search of souvenirs.

⑨ Blue Praha

Forget the traditional image of dust-collecting glass bowls and stemware. Blue Praha's *(see p88)* bold and quirky designs will light up your home like no old-fashioned glass can. Plus, the prices are low enough that you won't hesitate to use your purchases every day. You can also buy T-shirts and other gifts here.

Blue Praha

⑩ Náplavka Farmers' Market
MAP E6 ▪ Náplavka ▪ Open 8am–3pm Sat ▪ www.farmarsketrziste.cz

This riverfront food market is the place to be on summer Saturdays when the whole city seems to turn out to buy fresh produce, breads and meats. Even if you're not shopping, the atmosphere is infectious. Stroll the embankment and have a beer or coffee at the pop-up cafés. Follow the Vltava south beyond the National Theatre to find the market.

Náplavka Farmers' Market

TOP 10 Prague for Free

The medieval Astronomical Clock

1 Astronomical Clock
MAP L4 ■ Old Town Hall

Standing below the Gothic Old Town Hall, along with hundreds of fellow visitors, gawking up at the medieval clock (see p20) as it goes through its hourly procession (on the hour from 9am to 11pm) is a rite of passage. It is rather brief and admittedly under-whelming, but a must-see.

2 Prague Castle Grounds
MAP C2 ■ Prague Castle
■ www.hrad.cz

Visiting the permanent collections at Prague Castle can cost a king's ransom in entry fees. What many visitors don't realize is that it is totally free to enter the castle grounds and wander around to your heart's content. Don't miss the changing of the castle guard on the hour from 7am to 8pm (till 6pm in winter).

3 Old Jewish Cemetery
Spread across seven sites in Prague, the Jewish Museum is world class, with impressive exhibits and admission fees priced to match. If paying the full fee is beyond your budget, you can catch a small but worthwhile glimpse of the multitude of sombre tombstones in the Old Jewish Cemetery (see pp28–9) for

free through a small window set in the western wall of the cemetery on Ulice 17. listopadu.

4 John Lennon Wall
MAP D3 ■ Velkopřevorské náměstí, Malá Strana

This towering stretch of wall is covered with graffiti dedicated to Beatles frontman John Lennon. It is a relaxing – even spiritual – spot (see p93). Occasionally, buskers belt out their own renditions of "Yesterday" or "Imagine". Peaceful Kampa Island (see p94), a minute's walk to the east of the wall, is filled with hidden delights and well worth a wander.

The grave of Antonín Dvořák

5 Vyšehrad Cemetery
MAP B6 ■ Vyšehrad
■ www.praha-vysehrad.cz

The cemetery at Vyšehrad fortress (see p123) is the country's most prominent burial ground and is free to enter. Fans of classical music will enjoy looking for the graves of Antonín Dvořák and Bedřich Smetana, among others. Many of the tombstones are works of art in their own right.

6 Feed the Swans
MAP D2 ■ Malá Strana

Feeding the swans on the Vltava is a great activity for kids – although you'll have to shell out for for seed mix (not bread as it makes the swans ill). The classic spot is on the Malá Strana side, south of the Malostranská metro station.

Swans on the Vltava

7 Free Walking Tours
MAP P4 ■ Old Town
■ www.extravaganzafreetour.com

This is a great way to explore Prague with a guide. Free Prague Tours is run by licensed English-speaking guides who are also history buffs and people-orientated. Even with a generous tip at the end, you'll still save money. Tours normally begin at the Powder Gate at 11am and at Charles Bridge at 1pm.

8 View from Letná
MAP E1 ■ Greater Prague

Climb the steps at the northern end of Čechův most ("bridge" in Czech), north of Old Town Square for picture-postcard views of the Old Town and the bridges traversing the river below. Keep an eye out for the metronome (see p124) on the hill.

The Vltava, as seen from Letná

9 Wallenstein Garden
MAP D2 ■ Malá Strana ■ Open Apr–Oct: 7:30am–6pm Mon–Fri (from 10am Sat & Sun; Jun–Sep: to 7pm)
■ www.senat.cz

Malá Strana is full of Renaissance and Baroque gardens that levy a fee to enter but this lovely 17th-century garden (see p60) is free to the public. The palace (see p96), home to the Czech Senate, can also be visited.

10 Vojanovy sady
MAP D2 ■ U lužického semináře

Malá Strana has many green pockets, but Vojan's gardens top them all for their romantic charm. Tulip beds, flowering fruit trees and the occasional peacock add to the fairy-tale atmosphere.

TOP 10 BUDGET TIPS

A classical music performance

1 Opera and classical music in Prague is subsidized and tickets seldom cost more than a few thousand crowns.

2 Even if you're not a fan of multibunk hostels, consider renting a private single or double hostel room. Many hostels offer these at a fraction of the price they would cost in a hotel.

3 Time your stay to avoid the peak seasons around the Christmas, New Year and Easter holidays, when hotel rates go through the roof.

4 Consider renting an apartment rather than a hotel if you're staying for three days or longer. You'll not only save money but will have more privacy.

5 Buy a discounted 1-day or 3-day pass for Prague's public transport. These are valid for the metro, trams, buses, trains and boats, as well as transfers between them throughout the city. You'll save money and be spared the inconvenience of buying individual tickets for each journey.

6 When arriving by plane, take the municipal bus into town from the airport. A single Kč40 ticket can often get you very close to your hotel.

7 Resist the temptation to hop into a taxi. Most distances in the city are easily walkable, and public transport is reliable and cheap.

8 Eat out at lunchtime instead of dinner to take advantage of the popular three-course set menus.

9 Skip wine at meals in favour of beer. Czech wines can vary greatly in quality; the local beer is generally cheaper and excellent quality.

10 Seek out pubs in outlying districts like Žižkov, where a half-litre (pint) mug of beer can cost half the price it does in the centre.

Festivals

Performers on the streets during the Carnival at Masopust

Masopust
Shrove Tue

Locals dress up in masks, and sing and dance down the streets during this Czech carnival. Masopust translates to "meat-feasts" in Old Czech, alluding to the plethora of foodie feasts on offer as well. Celebrations are concentrated in the neighbourhood of Žižkov *(see p124)*.

② May Day
1 May

It is customary for couples to visit the statue of the Czech Romantic poet Karel Hynek Mácha on Petřín Hill *(see pp38–9)*. For others the national holiday is spent trying to forget the old obligatory Communist rallies.

③ Prague Spring International Music Festival
May–Jun

Bedřich Smetana's *Má vlast*, or *My Homeland (see p50)*, kicks off the annual three-week festival that draws classical music performers and fans from around the globe. The round of concerts closes with Beethoven's Ninth Symphony.

④ Tanec Praha
May, Jun

This international dance festival is on the verge of becoming something great. The local dance scene has greatly benefited from it, and audiences can now see contemporary productions all year round.

Karlovy Vary International Film Festival
Jul

Hobnob with the stars while you attend hundreds of screenings at this festival. Hundreds of partygoers turn the sleepy west Bohemian spa town, 130 km (81 miles) from Prague, upside down for nine days.

Performers at the Karlovy Vary

6 Street Theatre Festival
Jul

Za dveřmi (Behind the Door) is an international street art festival that presents drama, acrobatics, parades and juggling on the streets and squares of Prague.

7 Bohemia International Folklore Dance Festival
Aug

This festival has been a success since its first staging in 2005. It has now expanded beyond Prague, as DanceBohemia, and brings amateur folklore dance ensembles together from all around the world.

8 Prague Writer's Festival
Time varies every year

Salman Rushdie, Susan Sontag and Elie Wiesel are just some of the internationally acclaimed authors who have attended this annual event. The organizers often get grief for giving Czech writers short shrift.

A race at the Pardubice Steeplechase

9 Pardubice Steeplechase
Oct

The first steeplechase here was held in 1874. With 31 jumps stretching over 7 km (4 miles), this is one of the biggest in Europe.

10 Mikuláš, Vánoce, Silvestr
Dec

Christmas celebrations are largely devoid of religion, but the mulled wine starts flowing on St Nicholas's Day (6 December) and doesn't stop until the Christmas carp is all eaten and the New Year's Eve *(Silvestr)* fireworks arsenals are depleted.

TOP 10 NATIONAL HOLIDAYS

Traditional Czech Easter eggs

1 Renewal of the Independent Czech State
1 Jan
Marks the 1993 split of Czechoslovakia.

2 Easter Monday
Mar–Apr
Custom dictates that men give women a gentle whipping with a branch. There are calls to end this tradition.

3 Labour Day
1 May
Romantics lay flowers before the statue of Karel Hynek Mácha on Petřín Hill.

4 Day of Liberation
8 May
Plaques around town are adorned with flowers to remember those killed by the Germans in 1945.

5 Cyril and Methodius Day
5 Jul
The Greek missionaries *(see p45)* brought both Christianity and the Cyrillic alphabet to the Slavs.

6 Jan Hus Day
6 Jul
Czechs commemorate one of the greatest figures of Czech history *(see p43)*.

7 Czech Statehood Day
28 Sep
Bohemia's history is recalled on St Wenceslas Day, as most Czechs call it.

8 Independence Day
28 Oct
In 1918 Czechoslovakia declared itself independent of Austro-Hungary.

9 Day of the Fight for Freedom and Democracy
17 Nov
The Velvet Revolution anniversary is marked with candles and flowers.

10 Christmas
24–26 Dec
Streets fill with carp sellers and hedonists drinking mulled wine.

Prague
Area by Area

The Vltava flowing through
Prague's historical core

⁂🔟 Old Town

Prague's heart is a layered cake of history: the oldest of its buildings have double cellars, owing to a flood-prevention programme that buried the original streets 3 m (10 ft) beneath those that exist today. Architecturally, it embraces every epoch, from the Romanesque to the Brutalist style of the mid-1970s Kotva department store. Historically, the burghers of the Old Town (Staré Město) were ill at ease with the castle district, and vice versa, with the town being a bastion of Protestant feistiness. The Old Town is still livelier than Malá Strana and Hradčany, with cafés, clubs, restaurants and theatres that provide entertainment around the clock.

Municipal House

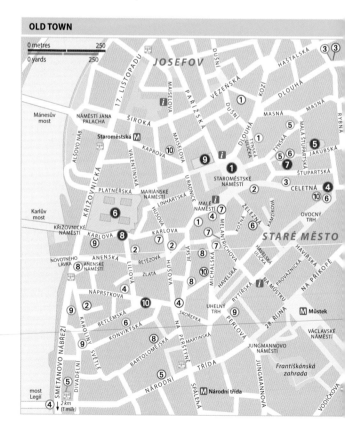

OLD TOWN

Old Town Square

1 Old Town Square

Over the centuries, this now peaceful square *(see pp18–21)* at the heart of the city has witnessed hundreds of executions, political capitulations and, more recently of course, riotous ice-hockey celebrations, a sport about which the Czechs are fanatical. Today, the action is more likely to come from the crowds of tourists and Praguers, enjoying a coffee or a glass of beer at one of the numerous pavement cafés. Dominated by the splendid Church of Our Lady before Týn, the square is always buzzing; in winter and summer, it's a wonderful place to watch the world go by.

2 Municipal House
MAP P3 ■ Náměstí Republiky 5 ■ Tours: 222 002101 ■ Adm ■ www. obecnidum.cz

National Revival artist Alfons Mucha was one of many to lend his talents to the Municipal House (Obecní dům), Prague's star Art Nouveau attraction. One of its most beautiful and striking features is Karel Špillar's mosaic above the main entrance, entitled *Homage to Prague*. It also has a firm place in history as it was from the Municipal House that Czechoslovakia was declared an independent state in 1918. Today, it is home to restaurants, cafés, exhibition halls, shops and the Prague Symphony Orchestra at the Smetana Hall *(see p66)*.

3 Powder Gate
MAP P4 ■ Náměstí Republiky ■ Open Apr–Sep: 10am–10pm (Oct & Mar: to 8pm; Nov–Feb: to 6pm) ■ Adm

In the 15th century, King Vladislav II laid the cornerstone for this tower at the city's eastern gate, intended to complement the Royal Court nearby. The name of this monument comes from its 17th-century role as a gunpowder store. The tower was damaged during Prussian attacks in 1757. The Neo-Gothic façade seen today, with its ornate sculptural decoration, dates from 1876.

Powder Gate

4 Celetná
MAP M4

The medieval route from the silver-mining town of Kutná Hora in Bohemia passed down the street known today as Celetná, through Old Town Square and on to Prague Castle. There is still a lot of traffic on the gently curving street today.

Traditional house sign, Celetná

5 Basilica of St James
MAP N3 ■ Malá Štupartská 6 ■ Open 9:30am–noon & 2–4pm daily (except Mon & during Mass) ■ praha. minorite.cz

The Gothic and Baroque interior wins the award for Prague's creepiest sanctuary. The church, founded in 1232 by Wenceslas I, is best known for the legend of the mummified arm (see p54) hanging above the door, but don't miss one of the organ recitals held here (see p67).

6 Clementinum
MAP K4 ■ Křížovnická 190, Mariánské náměstí 5 & Karlova 1 ■ 733 129252 ■ Open 10am–5pm daily (to 6pm Fri & Sat); concerts from 6pm daily (Nov–May: from 5pm) ■ Adm ■ www.klementinum.com

Built in the mid-17th century as a Jesuit college, the Clementinum now houses the National Library. Astronomer Johannes Kepler

Clementinum

(see p43) discovered the laws of planetary motion atop the Astronomical Tower. There is a beautiful Baroque library, and the Mirror Chapel hosts various concerts.

7 Ungelt
MAP M3

Also known as the Týn Courtyard, this was a fortified merchants settlement in the 10th century. The Baroque and Renaissance houses were completely renovated in the early 1990s, creating what is now one of the Old Town's most charming mercantile centres.

Buildings within the Ungelt complex

8 Karlova
MAP K4

You will inevitably get lost trying to follow Karlova street from the Old Town Square to Charles Bridge; relax and enjoy the bewildering, twisting alleys crammed with shops and cafés.

St Nicholas Cathedral, Old Town

⑨ St Nicholas Cathedral
MAP L3 ■ Staroměstské
náměstí ■ Open 10am–5pm daily
(from noon Sun) ■ Adm for concerts
■ www.svmikulas.cz

This Baroque jewel *(see p18)* started
life as a parish church. During World
War I, it was used as a garrison
church for Czech soldiers. It now
belongs to the Hussite Church and
also operates as a concert hall.

⑩ Bethlehem Square
MAP K5 ■ Chapel: Open
9am–6pm daily ■ Adm ■ www.
bethlehemchapel.eu

The 15th-century Catholic reformer
Jan Hus *(see p19)* preached in the
reconstructed chapel on the square's
north side. The church was converted
into apartments in the 18th century
but was lovingly restored to its
former state in the 1950s.

PRAGUE'S WALLS AND GATES

Prague's walls started going up in
the 13th century, protecting the new
settlement from the distant Tartars.
The town was accessible via wall gates.
As gradual developments in military
technology made walls and moats less
effective forms of defence, Praguers
found new uses for their fortifications.

The broad ramparts
became parks,
complete with
benches, lamps
and even cafés.
Prague kept the
habit of locking
its gates at night
well into the 19th
century, however.

Powder Gate detail

A STROLL AROUND THE OLD TOWN

[map showing: Old Town Square, Basilica of St James, Ungelt, Municipal House, Old Town Hall, Clementinum, Pasta Fresca, Celetná, Powder Gate, Karlova, U Zlatého tygra, Bethlehem Square]

▶ MORNING

After breakfast at the **Municipal
House** café *(see p85)*, take a
guided tour of the building, then
go and climb the **Powder Gate**
(see p85) next door for the views
before the caffeine wears off.

Wander down **Celetná**, ducking
through the arcade to Štupartská
and the **Basilica of St James**.
If you have at least 45 minutes
before the top of the hour, make
your way through the **Ungelt**
courtyard to the **Old Town Square**
(see p85). Join a tour of the **Old
Town Hall** and get a backstage
view of the Apostles' show on the
Astronomical Clock *(see pp20–21)*.
Otherwise, spend some time
shopping in the Ungelt, then join
the crowd below the clock outside
to see the spectacle.

For lunch, head slightly out of the
square to **Pasta Fresca** *(see p91)*
for delicious Italian fare.

AFTERNOON

Return to the Old Town Square and
do a quick circumnavigation, then
enter the meandering turns of
Karlova and wander leisurely past
the area's old buildings before
turning south to reach **Bethlehem
Square**. Take a tour of the lovely
Bethlehem Chapel. If you'd like
a little break, have a beer at the
legendary pub **U Zlatého tygra**
(see p90), a three-minute walk
north, then retrace your steps to
Karlova to visit the **Clementinum**.

After freshening up, take in
a concert or a performance
at the theatre. Curtains go up
around 7:30pm, so it is sensible
⬤ to dine afterwards.

See map on pp84–5 ⬅

Shops

1 Blue Praha
MAP L4 ■ Melantrichova 6

A dazzlingly different kind of glass shop (see p77) stocking modern, fun and quirky designs in bowls, knick-knacks, t-shirts and other tourist fare.

Glass being blown at Moser

2 Moser
MAP M4 ■ Staroměstské náměstí 15

Classic crystal and cut-glass objects produced by this well-known manufacturer. Even if you're not interested in a large vase or a crystal hedgehog, it's worth a look around.

3 Palladium
MAP P3 ■ Náměstí Republiky 1
■ www.palladiumpraha.cz

One of the most popular shopping destinations in downtown Prague, Palladium has 200 shops offering exciting shopping and dining experiences to visitors.

4 Erpet Bohemia Crystal
MAP L4 ■ Staroměstské náměstí 27

Located right across the Astronomical Clock, this megastore (see p76) has an exclusive collection of Bohemian crystal, art glass, fine costume jewelery, crystal figurines and much more. Friendly and attentive staff.

5 Material
MAP M3 ■ Týn 1, Ungelt

Czech tradition in designer crystal and glassware gets a modern makeover at this shop in the Ungelt courtyard. Admire the eye-catching stemware, vases, dishes and candle-holders, all presented in a space that fuses classical and modern design.

6 Botanicus
MAP M3 ■ Týn 2 & 3

The store's all-natural health and beauty products are produced at a "historic village" east of Prague; enquire about tours. Herbs, oils and other seasonings are also sold here (see p76).

7 Manufaktura
MAP L4 ■ Melantrichova 17

This is a one-stop shop (see p77) for your small souvenir needs, including Czech folk crafts and traditional wooden toys. In addition to these items, there are also naturally made cosmetics and toiletries featuring an odd assortment of ingredients, such as Czech beer, wine and thermal salt.

8 Art Deco
MAP L4 ■ Michalská 21

Come here (see p76) for a range of goods including handbags, jewellery, ceramics, glassware and vintage clothing inspired by the early 20th century.

9 Český Porcelán
MAP M5 ■ Perlová 1

Bohemian porcelain might not be as prestigious as Bohemian crystal, but it makes a pretty souvenir or present.

Porcelain jug at Český Porcelán

10 Hračky U zlatého lva
MAP N4 ■ Celetná 32

Kids will appreciate and enjoy the range of traditional wooden toys and other board games here (see p77).

Nightclubs

1 Kenton's
MAP L2 ▪ V Kolkovně 3
▪ 224 811165 ▪ www.kentons.cz

One of Prague's fancier bars, Kenton's *(see p75)* has a classy vibe with an elegant interior and a wooded counter. A good range of interesting cocktails.

2 Hemingway Bar
MAP J5 ▪ Karolíny Světlé 26
▪ 773 974764 ▪ www.hemingway bar.cz

Inspired by Ernest Hemingway, the great author and one of the most well-known bar lovers, this place *(see p75)* offers his favourite liquors such as Absinthe, a variety of rum, champagne and excels in mixology.

3 Roxy
MAP N2 ▪ Dlouhá 33
▪ www.roxy.cz

In addition to the best dance parties in town, this club *(see p68)* hosts experimental theatre and live bands.

4 Jazz Republic
MAP M6 ▪ Jilská 1a
▪ www.jazzrepublic.cz

One of Prague's top music clubs, Jazz Republic features live jazz, funk, blues, dance, Latin, fusion or world music seven nights a week.

5 Vagon
MAP L6 ▪ Národní třída 25

One of the originals for exciting live music, this place hosts blues or rock bands most nights, with a mix of well-known and unsigned acts.

Performers at Vagon

The AghaRTA Jazz Centrum club

6 AghaRTA Jazz Centrum
MAP M4 ▪ Železná 16
▪ www.agharta.cz

Named after Miles Davis's seminal album from the 1970s and opened the day after his death, this club has daily performances by top Czech musicians and hosts the annual AghaRTA Prague Jazz Festival.

7 Black Angel's
MAP L4 ▪ Staroměstské náměstí 29 ▪ 224 213807
▪ www.blackangelsbar.com

Designed in the style of a Prohibtion era speakeasy, this attractive bar *(see p75)* offers creative drinks and cocktails.

8 Friends
MAP K6 ▪ Bartolomějská 11
▪ www.friendsclub.cz

Prague's best gay cocktail bar has a steady following among expat and local men and is always welcoming towards new visitors. The owner Michael will tell you what's what.

9 Zlatý Strom
MAP K4 ▪ Karlova 6
▪ www.zlatystrom.com

Enjoy unusual views of the Prague night sky through the glass ceilings of this subterranean club. There are two dance floors inside.

10 Caffrey's
MAP M3 ▪ Staroměstské náměstí 10 ▪ www.caffreys.cz

This lively Irish bar is one of the most popular in town. The beer terrace at front of the pub offers the perfect setting to enjoy drinks during summer.

See map on pp84–5

Cafés and Pubs

① Café Obecní dům
MAP P3 ■ Náměstí Republiky 5

Covered in Art Nouveau splendour, this café at the Municipal House glitters. Stop in for breakfast before setting off for a day exploring the Old Town and its sights.

② U Tří Růží
MAP L5 ■ Husova 10 ■ 601 588281 ■ www.u3r.cz

This Old-Prague brewery and restaurant (see p75) has a unique charm and combines original ingredients and traditional craftsmanship of brewing to offer a range of beers.

③ Lokál Dlouháááá
MAP N2 ■ Dlouhá 33 ■ 734 283874

Rumoured to serve the city's freshest Pilsner Urquell beer, delivered to the door in big tanks, this pub also serves better-than-average traditional Czech pub meals – think goulash and roast pork – at very reasonable prices. Advance booking is essential.

④ Terasa U Prince
MAP L4 ■ Staroměstské náměstí 29 ■ 737 261842

Visit this café-cum-restaurant on the lovely rooftop terrace of Hotel U Prince for a truly unforgettable dining experience.

⑤ Café Slavia
MAP J6 ■ Národní třída 1 ■ 224 218493 ■ www.cafeslavia.cz

Set in the historical centre of Prague, this traditional café (see p74) offers Czech and international cuisine that include salads, fish and meat specialities. Guests are also serenaded by live piano music in the evenings.

⑥ Grand Café Orient
MAP N4 ■ Ovocný trh 19 ■ 224 224240 ■ www.grandcafeorient.cz

With its unique Cubist style decor, the specialities at this elegant café (see p75) include the traditional Czech pastry, Kubistický věneček.

⑦ U Zlatého tygra
MAP L4 ■ Husova 17 ■ 222 221111 ■ No credit cards ■ www.uzlatehotygra.cz

Located in the heart of the Old Town, this pub (see p74) is renowned for its old world charm and Pilsner beer.

⑧ Prague Beer Museum
MAP J5 ■ Smetanovo nábřeží 22 ■ 732 330912

This is one of the three branches of this popular pub with around 30 Czech beers on tap.

⑨ Atmosphere
MAP J5 ■ Smetanovo náb. 14

This café, pub and restaurant offers its customers tank beer, Italian and Czech wines, plus a varied menu that includes Czech dishes.

⑩ Café Ebel
MAP L3 ■ Kaprova 11

You won't find a better cup of coffee in the city than at Ebel, which uses beans from all over the world. Not far from the Old Town Square.

Rooftop, Terasa U Prince

Restaurants

① Maitrea
M3 ▪ Týnská ulička 6 ▪ 221 7116317 ▪ www.restaurace-maitrea.cz ▪ Ⓚ Ⓚ Ⓚ

Located just off the Old Town Square, Maitrea is an excellent vegetarian and vegan restaurant which serves traditional (but meat free) Czech fare alongside Mexican, Thai and other international dishes.

Elegant interior of Maitrea

② Wine O'Clock
K4 ▪ Liliová 1069 ▪ 773 201216 ▪ www.wineoclockprague.com ▪ Ⓚ Ⓚ

Enjoy tasty Italian small plates, from bruschetta *pomodoro* to aubergine *parmiggiana*, with a glass of wine.

③ Pasta Fresca
MAP M4 ▪ Celetná 11 ▪ 224 230244 ▪ Ⓚ Ⓚ Ⓚ

Chef Tomáš Mykytyn makes regional Italian dishes with seasonal ingredients. Sommeliers are on hand to guide diners through the wine menu.

④ V Zátiší
MAP K5 ▪ Liliová 1 ▪ 222 221155 ▪ Ⓚ Ⓚ Ⓚ

Enjoy modern and unconventional versions of traditional Czech and Indian dishes at this well-established fine dining restaurant *(see p72)*.

⑤ Divinis
MAP M3 ▪ Týnská 21 ▪ 770 682105 ▪ Closed Sun ▪ Ⓚ Ⓚ Ⓚ

This high-end wine bar and restaurant manages to balance a modern feel with a traditional Italian atmosphere.

PRICE CATEGORIES
For a three-course meal for one with half a bottle of wine (or equivalent meal), taxes and extra charges.

Ⓚ under Kč500 Ⓚ Ⓚ Kč500–Kč1,000
Ⓚ Ⓚ Ⓚ over Kč1,000

Good-quality wines complement the classic Sicilian specialities.

⑥ Sad Man's Tongue
MAP K6 ▪ Konviktská 7 ▪ No credit cards ▪ www.sadmanstongue.com ▪ Ⓚ

This popular bar and bistro serves up a big helping of Americana in the heart of Prague. Expect fully-loaded burgers, buffalo wings and nachos.

⑦ Bistro Monk
MAP L4 ▪ Michalská 20 ▪ 777 119785 ▪ Ⓚ Ⓚ

Prepared from fresh, local produce, the food at Bistro Monk is simple and delicious. The pancakes with blueberry sauce are a must-try.

⑧ Hosarowa
MAP L5 ▪ Jilská 6 ▪ 220 921 499 ▪ https://hosarowa.business.site ▪ Ⓚ Ⓚ

Come here for Prague's best Korean barbecue, along with other delicious Korean classics like bibimbap and *garak-guksu*.

⑨ Století
MAP N2 ▪ Karolíny Světlé 21 ▪ 222 220008 ▪ Ⓚ Ⓚ

Enjoy dishes named after Czech artists, writers and singers in a simple but stylish dining room. The menu has a good list of vegetarian options.

⑩ Plzeňská restaurace Obecní dům
MAP P3 ▪ Náměstí Republiky 5 ▪ 222 002780 ▪ Ⓚ Ⓚ

Classic Czech dishes are served in a lively setting here *(see p73)*. The extensive à la carte menu features dishes such as roast duck and grilled ribs.

See map on pp84–5

🔟 Malá Strana

Founded in 1257, Malá Strana (the Little Quarter) is built on the slopes below the castle hill with magnificent views across the river to the Old Town. Floods, fires and war kept construction going on the Vltava's left bank; very few of the original Romanesque and Gothic buildings remain. During the reign of the Habsburgs, grand palaces were built in Baroque style, and today many of these serve as parliament or government buildings and embassies. The area is an enclave of parks, cafés, winding streets and unassuming churches.

Malá Strana tower, Charles Bridge

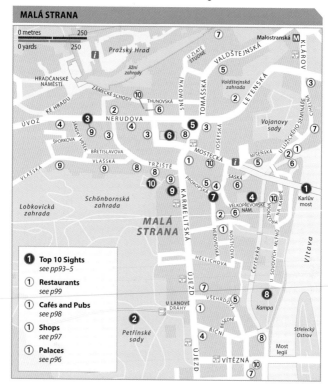

MALÁ STRANA

1	Top 10 Sights see pp93–5
1	Restaurants see p99
1	Cafés and Pubs see p98
1	Shops see p97
1	Palaces see p96

A scenic view of the Vltava and Charles Bridge, as seen from Petřín Hill

① Charles Bridge

For almost all visitors to Prague, this spectacular Gothic bridge *(see pp22–3)*, crossing the Vltava from the castle complex to the Old Town, remains their most memorable image of the city long after they have returned home.

② Petřín Hill

A more than welcome respite from the tiny, generally crowded streets in the city below is this sprawling park looking down over spires and rooftops. Enjoy the views all the way up the hill by taking the funicular *(see pp38–9)*.

The Golden Horseshoe, Nerudova 34

③ Nerudova
MAP C2

The 19th-century Czech writer and poet Jan Neruda (1834–91) lived in the House of the Two Suns, at the top of the street that now bears his name. Lined with former palaces, Nerudova street leads uphill from Malostranské náměstí, its many winding side streets leading visitors up to Prague Castle *(see pp12–15)*.

Traditionally an artists' quarter, the street is worth exploring for its many craft shops and galleries. It is also home to one of the most concentrated collections of historic house signs *(see pp52–3)* in the city.

④ John Lennon Wall
MAP D3 ■ Velkopřevorské náměstí

Prague hippies and the secret police once waged a long-running paint battle here, as the latter constantly tried to eradicate the graffiti artists' work *(see p78)*. The original artwork, created by students after Lennon's assassination, has been painted over many times, but the John Lennon Peace Club still gathers annually at this self-made shrine to sing the former Beatle's praises – and his songs.

Artwork on the John Lennon Wall

Trams at Malostranské náměstí

⑤ Malostranské náměstí
MAP C2

The hectic traffic that now detracts from the beauty of Malá Strana's main square seems historically fitting – in the past it has been witness to innumerable destructive fires, revolutions and executions (during the days when a gallows stood here). St Nicholas Church and the adjoining Jesuit college dominate the centre of the square, while lovely Neo-Classical palace arcades and restaurants line the perimeter.

⑥ St Nicholas Church
MAP C2 ▪ Malostranské náměstí ▪ Open Mar–Oct: 9am–5pm daily (Nov–Feb: to 4pm) ▪ Adm ▪ www.stnicholas.cz

In the early 18th century, Jesuits constructed this stunning example of Baroque architecture on the site of a former Gothic parish. This prominent Prague landmark was designed by the acclaimed father and son Baroque architects, Christoph and Kilian Dientzenhofer, while other leading artists adorned the interior with exquisite carvings, statues and frescoes. From the 1950s the clock tower often served as an observation and spying point for the state security. For an extra fee, you can climb the tower for a memorable view over the orange rooftops of Malá Strana.

THE HEDONISTS' QUARTER

The district of Malá Strana became something of a party town for the Viennese nobility during the 18th century. Wolfgang Amadeus Mozart strayed from the straight and narrow here, as did Casanova – in his sunset years, the ageing playboy penned his memoirs at the palace that is now home to the British Embassy. The trend continues today, with Prague's youth gathering in the park on Kampa Island to play music, smoke and drink.

⑦ Maltézské náměstí
MAP C3

The Knights of Malta once had an autonomous settlement here, and the square still bears their name. Search for the Bench of Václav Havel in the centre of the square. Hiding just a few steps from the square to the east is the 12th-century Church of Our Lady below the Chain, whose name refers to the chain used in the Middle Ages to close the monastery gatehouse.

⑧ Kampa Island
MAP D3–4

The tiny Čertovka (Devil's Canal) that separates Kampa from Malá Strana was once the town's "laundry", milling area and, in the 17th century, home to a thriving pottery industry. A popular park now covers the island's *(see p60)* southern end, while the northern half is home to elegant embassies, restaurants and hotels.

Kampa Island and the Čertovka canal

Church of Our Lady Victorious

(9) Church of Our Lady Victorious

MAP C3 ■ Karmelitská 9 ■ Open 8:30am–6pm Mon–Sat (to 8pm Sun) ■ Museum of the Infant Jesus of Prague: 9:30am–5:30pm Mon–Sat, 1–6pm Sun

Also known as the Church of the Infant Jesus of Prague, Prague's first Baroque church (1611) got its name and its Catholic outlook after the Battle of White Mountain (see p42). Visitors flock to see the church's miracle-working statue of the infant Christ (see p44).

(10) Vrtba Garden

MAP C3 ■ Karmelitská 25 ■ Open Apr–Oct: 10am–6pm daily ■ www.vrtbovska.cz

Enjoy magnificient views of Prague Castle and the Mala Strana from the highest point of this beautiful Baroque garden laid out by architect František Maximilián Kaňka in about 1720.

A DAY IN MALÁ STRANA

Wallenstein Garden
Malostranské náměstí
Vojanovy sady
Nerudova
St Nicholas Church
U Malého Glena
Vrtba Garden
Church of Our Lady Victorious
John Lennon Wall
Maltézské náměstí
Kampa Island

MORNING

You can approach the Little Quarter from the Old Town as royal processions once did, by crossing Charles Bridge (see p93), or you can save your energy for the day ahead, and start from the top of the hill and walk down. Get to **Nerudova** (see p93) from one of the many side streets leading from Hradčany and stroll down, window shopping at the many craft outlets on your way. Don't worry if you stray off the beaten path; as long as you go downhill, you'll end up at the area's central hub, **Malostranské náměstí**. Here, spend at least an hour savouring one of the city's most spectacular buildings, **St Nicholas Church**. Pause for lunch at one of the many pleasant cafés on Malostranské náměstí.

AFTERNOON

After lunch, take Tomášská to the **Wallenstein Garden** (see p60). Tiptoe through the tulips at **Vojanovy sady** (see p79) and continue down U lužického semináře under Charles Bridge and onto the lovely **Kampa Island**. Explore the island, then head off to check the writing on the **John Lennon Wall** (see p93) before visiting the **Church of Our Lady Victorious** and finally enjoy the magnificent evening views from the highest point of **Vrtba Garden**.

In the evening, relax at the Bench of Václav Havel in the middle of Maltézské náměstí, or head to **U Malého Glena** (see p98) to relax while listening to jazz and blues.

See map on p92 ←

Palaces

1 Nostitz Palace
MAP D3 ■ Maltézské náměstí 1

Take in the restoration work at this 17th-century palace while enjoying a chamber music concert. The palace now serves as the seat of the Czech Ministry of Culture.

2 Thun-Hohenstein Palace
MAP C2 ■ Nerudova 20

Façade of the Nostitz Palace

The Kolowrat family's heraldic eagles support the portal of this palace. Built by Giovanni Santini-Aichel in 1721, the building is now home to the Italian Embassy.

3 Liechtenstein Palace
MAP C2 ■ Malostranské náměstí 13 ■ www.amu.cz

Originally several different houses, the Liechtenstein Palace fused in the 16th century. Today, it is home to Prague's Academy of Music and hosts concerts and recitals.

4 Morzin Palace
MAP C2 ■ Nerudova 5

The two giant Moors (hence Morzin) bearing up the Romanian Embassy's façade are said to wander about Malá Strana streets at night.

Wallenstein Palace ceiling frescoes

5 Wallenstein Palace
MAP D2 ■ Valdštejnské náměstí 4 ■ Open 10am–6pm Sat ■ Adm ■ www.senat.cz

General Wallenstein pulled out all the stops creating what is essentially a monument to himself. On the palace's frescoes, the Thirty Years' War commander had himself depicted as both Achilles and Mars.

6 Buquoy Palace
MAP D3 ■ Velkopřevorské náměstí 2

This pink stucco palace and the John Lennon Wall are separated by only a few steps, but they are miles apart aesthetically. The French Ambassador helped preserve the graffiti opposite his offices in the 1980s.

7 Michna Palace
MAP C4 ■ Újezd 40

Francesco Caratti modelled this palace on Versailles in the 17th century. It is home to the Sokol Physical Culture Movement.

8 Schönborn Palace
MAP C3 ■ Tržiště 15

Count Colloredo-Mansfeld owned the palace in the 17th century: having lost a leg in the Thirty Years' War, he had the stairs rebuilt so he could ride his horse into the building. Czechoslovakia's first ambassador to the United States sold the palace to the US government in 1925.

9 Lobkowicz Palace (Převorovských)
MAP B3 ■ Vlašská 19

Home to the German Embassy. In 1989 hundreds of East Germans found their way to the West by scrambling over the back fence of this embassy building.

10 Kaunitz Palace
MAP C3 ■ Mostecká 15

The Yugoslav (now Serbian) Embassy sat quietly in its pink and yellow stucco palace for more than 300 years until war made it a popular spot for protests.

Shops

1 Bel Art Gallery
MAP C3 ■ Karmelitská 26

This small fine art gallery and shop, set in a 17th-century building, sells contemporary paintings, sculptures and ceramic works from more than 30 acclaimed artists. International shipping is available.

2 Shakespeare a Synové
MAP D3 ■ U lužického semináře 10

This bookstore specializes in foreign books and several titles in English, German and French. It offers a space for literary readings and discussions.

3 Muzeum Slivovice R. Jelínek
MAP D2 ■ U Lužického semináře 48
■ www.muzeumslivovice.cz

Head to the shop of this distillery museum to pick up a bottle of *slivovice*, a traditional Czech plum spirit. Book a tasting to sample it before buying.

Products in Obchod vším možným

4 Obchod vším možným
MAP B2 ■ Nerudova 45

Just under New Castle Steps, this small shop sells original Czech puppets, gifts, toys, ceramics, jewellery, art and enamel tableware.

5 Artěl
MAP D3 ■ U lužického semináře 7

This store *(see p76)* is known for exquisite mouth-blown and hand-engraved glassware and crystalware for decor of unique design motifs.

Květinářstvi u Červeného lva

6 Květinářstvi u Červeného lva
MAP D3 ■ Saská

It appears as if a jungle is sprouting from the hole in the wall that is the Flowershop at the Red Lion. Spruce up your apartment or hotel room with their unique arrangements.

7 Perníkový panáček
MAP D2 ■ Cihelna 2a

Located near the entrance to the Franz Kafka museum, this charming little side-street bakery has all manner of gingerbread creations, which make for great gifts.

8 Malostranské starožitnictví
MAP C2 ■ Malostranské náměstí 28

This antiques store is a veritable treasure trove of jewellery, watches, porcelain objects, silverware, coins and photographs. It also sells larger items, such as musical instruments.

9 Designum Gallery
MAP C2 ■ Nerudova 27

This design boutique offers the works of up-and-coming artists apart from the established brands and designers. The highlights at the boutique include glass, porcelain as well as contemporary jewellery.

10 Orel and Friends
MAP C2 ■ Nerudova 6

A wide selection of traditional Czech crafts including ceramics, jewellery, handbags, leather-bound books and more, are available at this unique store.

See map on p92

Cafés and Pubs

1 Bakeshop Little Bakery
MAP D2 ■ U lužického semináře 22

Close to Charles Bridge and located opposite a park, this little bakery serves pastries, breads, quiches and desserts. They also have a daily changing menu of fresh juices, smoothies and a homemade soup served with croutons.

The lovely Café Kafíčko

2 Café Kafíčko
MAP C3 ■ Maltézské náměstí 15

This café, with its excellent coffee and homemade cakes, proves to be the perfect getaway from the cold of the winter or the summer crowds.

3 Baráčnická rychta
MAP C3 ■ Tržiště 23

This wood-panelled beer hall, housed in a Modernist 1930s building, is a little piece of traditional Czech Republic in Malá Strana.

4 Cukrkávalimonáda
MAP C3 ■ Lázeňská 7

Located opposite the entrance to the Church of Our Lady the Chain, this popular little patisserie is all about three things: *cukr* (sugar), *káva* (coffee) and *limonáda* (lemonade).

5 Alebrijes Bar Bar
MAP D4 ■ Všehrdova 17

Come to this cosy restaurant and bar for a relaxed meal with friends and family, and enjoy traditional Mexican drinks and cuisine.

6 U Kocoura
MAP C2 ■ Nerudova 2

You might think the regulars at this pub on Malá Strana's main drag would be used to tourists by now, but don't be surprised if every face turns to meet you. Serves excellent Pilsner.

7 Kofarna Café
MAP D4 ■ Zborovská 84/60

In addition to excellent coffee, Kofarna offers many plant-based food options too. Try the famous Israeli hummus.

8 Café Bella Vida
MAP D4 ■ Malostranské nábřezí 3

This café serves its own coffee blend as well as delectable mini-desserts and sandwiches. Sit in the cosy garden and enjoy the beautiful views of Charles Bridge and Prague Castle.

9 U Malého Glena
MAP C3 ■ Karmelitská 23
■ www.malyglen.cz

Prague's smallest jazz venue, "At Small Glen's" *(see p69)*, also has a cosy restaurant where you can enjoy a variety of food and brunch at weekends.

10 The Wall Pub
MAP D3 ■ Hroznová 495

Less than a minute's walk from Lennon Wall, this pub is all about celebrating the legendary singer. Enjoy steaks and burgers in the garden.

Interior of The Wall Pub

Restaurants

PRICE CATEGORIES
For a three-course meal for one with half a bottle of wine (or equivalent meal), taxes and extra charges.

Kč under Kč500 KčKč Kč500–Kč1,000
KčKčKč over Kč1,000

1 Cantina

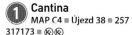

MAP C4 ■ Újezd 38 ■ 257 317173 ■ KčKč

Perhaps the best Mexican food in Prague. The fajitas are great; choose from chicken, beef, pork or shrimp. Book ahead.

2 Augustine Restaurant

MAP D2 ■ Letenská 12/33 ■ 266 112282 ■ KčKčKč

This gorgeous restaurant *(see p73)* serves European cuisine prepared with seasonal ingredients and a wide selection of drinks.

3 Malostranská Beseda

MAP C2 ■ Malostranské náměstí 21 ■ 257 409112 ■ KčKč

Set in an elegant building in the heart of Little Quarter, this cosy place serves traditional Czech food and beer.

4 Czech Slovak Restaurant

MAP C4 ■ Újezd 20 ■ KčKč

This place brings traditional Czech and Slovak dishes into the 21st century in an artistic fashion. There is also a wide selection of drinks available.

5 Ichnusa Botega Bistro

MAP D4 ■ Plaská 5 ■ 605 375012 ■ KčKčKč

An inviting and family-run bistro *(see p73)* which offers a delicious range of Sardinian dishes paired with drinks.

6 Kampa Park

MAP D3 ■ Na Kampě 8b ■ 296 826102 ■ KčKčKč

This top riverside restaurant *(see p72)* has three terraces and a winter garden. It serves a mix of Continental classics and fusion cuisine.

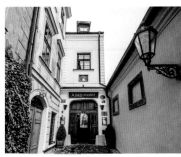

Façade of Terasa U Zlaté studně

7 Terasa U Zlaté studně

MAP C2 ■ U Zlaté studně 4 ■ 257 533322 ■ KčKčKč

With its picturesque views, elegant decor and classic cuisine, this fine dining restaurant *(see p73)* offers the perfect setting to celebrate special occasions with friends and family.

8 Coda Restaurant

MAP C3 ■ Tržiště 9 ■ 225 334761 ■ KčKčKč

Enjoy the stunning views from the rooftop terrace on the Aria Hotel while you sample delicious Czech dishes from the tasting menu.

9 St Martin

MAP C3 ■ Vlašská 7 ■ 257 219728 ■ www.stmartin.cz ■ KčKč

Try traditional Czech dishes alongside Asian twists on American classics (like the kimchi burger).

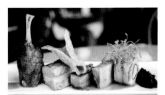

Appetizers at Café Savoy

10 Café Savoy

MAP C4 ■ Vítězná 5 ■ 731 136144 ■ KčKčKč

This feels just like a Prague café should, with high ceilings, elegant fixtures and huge windows. It has a standard as well as gourmet menu.

See map on p92 ←

Prague Castle and Hradčany

Founded by Prince Bořivoj in the 9th century, Prague Castle and its attendant cathedral tower overlook the city from the long hill known as Hradčany. The surrounding town was founded in 1320, becoming home to servants' hovels and, after the cataclysmic fire of 1541, grand palaces. Renaissance and Baroque reconstructions in the area created much of what visitors see today. The Loreta shrine to the Virgin Mary demonstrated the growing importance of Prague to the church. At the castle, primitive defences were removed, making room for gardens, parade grounds and the other needs of a modern empire. When the Habsburgs removed the imperial seat to Vienna, Hradčany seemed to become preserved in time, saving it from the ravages of war and modernization. The area abounds with interesting sights for art and history lovers, as well as romantic hidden lanes and parks – in short, a total expression of the Czech nation's shifting epochs and politics.

PRAGUE CASTLE AND HRADČANY

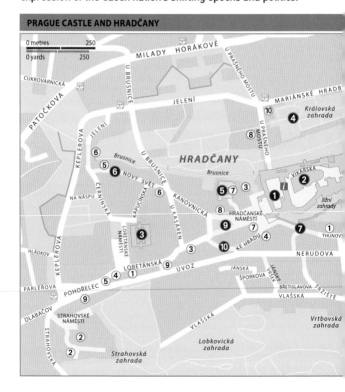

Prague Castle rising above the town

1 Prague Castle

The first and main focus of most tourists' visit to the city of Prague is the majestically located and architecturally varied castle complex (see pp12–15). Its determined survival in the face of an often turbulent history seems only to heighten the castle's lure for tourists. Despite its medieval appearance, it is still as much of a political stronghold as it has always been, and currently serves as the office of the country's president.

2 St Vitus Cathedral

The Gothic splendour of St Vitus's (see pp16–17) spires can be seen from almost every vantage point in the city, but don't miss the opportunity to see its beautiful stained-glass windows and imposing gargoyles up close.

3 Loreta

The onion-domed white towers of this Baroque 17th-century church (see pp26–7) complex are like something out of a fairy tale.

4 Royal Garden

MAP C1 ■ U Prašného mostu
■ Open Apr–Oct: 10am–dusk daily
■ www.hrad.cz

This garden was originally laid out in 1534 by Ferdinand I. Although today's visitors may regret the disappearance of the maze and the pineapple trees that once featured here, they are likely to appreciate the absence of Rudolf II's freely roaming lions and tigers. In the English-style garden are the former presidential residence (the First Lady didn't like it), the sgraffitoed Ball Game Hall and Queen Anne's Summer Palace (Letohrádek královny Anny), also known as the Belvedere.

Flowerbeds at the Royal Garden

1 Top 10 Sights
see pp101–103

1 Restaurants
see p105

1 Cafés and Pubs
see p104

STAG MOAT

When the Stag Moat was not fulfilling its defensive duties, Prague's rulers used it as a hunting park. Rudolf II is said to have been particularly fond of chasing deer around the narrow, wooded gorge with his pet lions. The Powder Bridge's earthworks were excavated to permit pedestrians access to both halves of the moat.

5 Sternberg Palace
MAP B2 ■ Hradčanské náměstí 15

This fine Baroque building, (see p48) dating from 1698, houses the National Gallery's (see p48) collection of European art from the classical to the Baroque. Spread over three floors, it is without doubt the country's best collection from the period. Its highlights include works by Rubens, Rembrandt and El Greco.

A Bronzino painting, Sternberg Palace

6 Nový Svět
MAP A2

Nestled below Loreta (see pp26–7), at the head of the Stag Moat, is Nový Svět (New World), the best street in town for a romantic stroll. The picturesque low houses were built in the 17th century to replace slums built for castle workers after their houses burned down in 1541. They have been spruced up, but are otherwise unspoiled. In defiance of their poverty, the inhabitants of these cottages chose to use golden signs to identify their modest houses – visitors will see depictions of a golden pear, a grape and an acorn. Rudolf II's choleric astronomer Tycho Brahe (see p43) lived at No. 1 and apparently found the noise of nearby church bells insufferable.

7 New Castle Steps
MAP C2

The Royal Route, established in the 15th century for the coronation of George of Poděbrady, covered the distance from the Municipal House on Náměstí Republiky (see p85) to the castle. The last stretch climbed the hill here at the Zámecké schody, although the original steps were reconstructed during Empress Maria Theresa's Hradčany renovation in the 18th century.

Charming houses lining tranquil Nový Svět

8 Old Castle Steps
MAP D2

The comparatively gentle slope of the Staré zámecké schody – the castle's "back door" entrance – leads from the Malostranská metro to the citadel's eastern gate. Local artists and artisans line the steps, selling everything from watercolour prints to polished stones.

The grandiose Archbishop's Palace

9 Hradčanské náměstí
MAP B2

Many visitors enter this square backwards, trying to fit St Vitus's spires into their photographs. Tear your eyes away from the castle's western face and you'll see, among other Renaissance buildings, the colourful Archbishop's Palace and the Schwarzenberg Palace opposite, housing the Bohemian Baroque art of the National Gallery (see p48). In the green centre is a plague column from 1726; opposite the castle is the Toskánský Palace, now part of the Ministry of Foreign Affairs.

10 Radnické schody
MAP B2

The Courthouse Steps lead from Hradčany's former mayoral residence, now the hotel Zlatá Hvězda, to the old courthouse at Loretánská 1. At the bottom are two statues – on the left is St John of Nepomuk and on the right St Joseph with the infant Jesus in Renaissance garb. There are more steps than is immediately apparent, making the pub halfway up a convenient stopping-off point.

A DAY IN HRADČANY

▶ MORNING

Start your day with a brisk climb up the **New Castle Steps**, then take a leisurely stroll through the scenic grounds. When you're ready, leave the castle behind and walk west through **Hradčanské náměstí**; time your exit for the Changing of the Guard at noon. Next, head to the Schwarzenberg Palace, set amid the Renaissance structures that surround the square, and take time to admire some Baroque Czech art. Alternatively, treat yourself to the Old Masters collection at **Sternberg Palace**.

Now walk up **Loretánská** to **Loretánské náměstí**, where you'll find the vast Černín Palace staring down at **Loreta** (see p101). Explore the pilgrimage site and its odd gallery of saints before having lunch at the simple Kavárna Nový Svět (see p104).

AFTERNOON

Exit Loretánské náměstí past the Capuchin monastery and follow Černínská downhill, pausing on **Nový Svět** lane. Coo over the street's charming piebald houses and follow Kanovnická street back to Hradčanské náměstí.

The rest of the afternoon will be taken up with a tour of the unmissable **Prague Castle** (see p101), **St Vitus Cathedral** (see p101) and the myriad of other attractions in the castle complex.

To end your sightseeing day in Hradčany, find your way back to the famed pub **U Černého vola** (see p104) at Loretánské náměstí 1 for a pickled sausage and a generous mug of beer.

See map on pp100–101 ←

Cafés and Pubs

① U Černého vola
MAP A2 ■ Loretánské nám. 1

"At the Black Ox" is one of the original Old Prague beerhalls. Watching the regulars knock back litres of beer, you can guess why it's so popular.

② Pivovar Strahov
MAP A3 ■ Strahovské nádvoří 301

Located in the Strahov Monastery founded by Vladislav II in 1142, this place brews 25 delicious beers. The Saint Norbert is highly recommended.

③ Na Baště
MAP B2 ■ Zahrada na Baště, Prague Castle ■ 224 373599

This is an out-of-the-way, peaceful café in the Gardens on the Bastion, which were designed by Slovenian architect Jože Plečnik. Rest over tea or coffee and light snacks here.

④ Starbucks Pražský hrad
MAP B2 ■ Hradčanské náměstí - Kajetánka

Sip an espresso on the rooftop while peering at Prague through one of the telescopes. The quiet patio has large tables where you can lunch and plan your visit to the castle next door.

⑤ Kavárna Nový Svět
MAP A2 ■ Nový Svět 2 ■ 242 430700 ■ Closed Mon

Small family café hidden in a picturesque street. Try soup or salad for lunch, or just sit with a good cup of coffee and enjoy the atmosphere.

⑥ Romantik Hotel U Raka
MAP A2 ■ Černínská 10

The Hotel U Raka at the far western end of Nový Svět is a striking half-timbered building, an unusual sight in the urban Czech Republic. Enjoy a coffee in cosy surroundings – there is an open fire in winter.

⑦ Café Šternberk
MAP B2 ■ Hradčanské nám. 15

Situated in the Sternberg Palace, this is a good spot to enjoy a cup of coffee and a baguette or a light meal after visiting the castle and before heading off to visit the other palaces nearby.

⑧ Gallery Café
MAP B2 ■ U Prašného mostu 53

This café and gallery is situated at the Powder Bridge in the former Jízdárna (Riding School) building. Outdoor seating is available in good weather and offers stunning views of Prague Castle and Stag Moat.

⑨ Café Melvin
MAP A3 ■ Pohořelec 8

Set in a 15th-century house at the beginning of the Royal Route, this café serves a range of beverages, home-made desserts and sandwiches.

⑩ Lobkowicz Palace Café
MAP C2 ■ Jiřská 3

This pleasant restaurant offers light lunches and suppers with a view of the city. The café in the courtyard is a good place to end your tour of the castle.

Lobkowicz Palace Café balcony

Restaurants

PRICE CATEGORIES

For a three-course meal for one with half a bottle of wine (or equivalent meal), taxes and charges.

Ⓚ under Kč500   ⒦Ⓚ Kč500–Kč1,000
Ⓚ ⒦Ⓚ over Kč1,000

1 U Krále Brabantského
MAP C2 ▪ Thunovská 15
▪ 602 524725 ▪ www.krcma
brabant.cz ▪ Ⓚ Ⓚ

Meat lovers will enjoy this medieval-themed restaurant in a genuinely historic setting.

2 Peklo
MAP A3 ▪ Strahovské nadvoří 1
▪ 220 516652 ▪ Ⓚ Ⓚ

Continental dining in a grotto under the Strahov Monastery. Traditional Czech meals include golden-roasted pork knee.

3 U Císařů
MAP B2 ▪ Loretánská 5 ▪ 220 518484 ▪ Ⓚ Ⓚ Ⓚ

The restaurant "At the Emperors" serves traditional specialities and international favourites. The decor includes fine pewter tableware collections, hunting weapons and blacksmith bellows.

4 U ševce Matouše
MAP A2 ▪ Loretánské náměstí 4
▪ 220 514536 ▪ Ⓚ Ⓚ

"At the Cobbler Matouš", in a cosy, low, vaulted room, has made an art of melting cheese on beefsteaks.

5 Malý Buddha
MAP A3 ▪ Úvoz 46 ▪ 220 513894 ▪ No credit cards ▪ Ⓚ Ⓚ

The "Little Buddha" serves a wide range of potent teas and Vietnamese food.

6 Plzeňka Nový Svět
MAP B2 ▪ Nový Svět 77
▪ 773 781010 ▪ Ⓚ Ⓚ

This restaurant serves delicious Czech and international dishes, and is immensely popular with locals and tourists alike.

7 Kuchyň
MAP B2 ▪ Hradčanské náměstí 1 ▪ 736 152891 ▪ https://kuchyn.ambi.cz ▪ Ⓚ Ⓚ

This restaurant may no longer offer its USP (allowing diners into the kitchen to sniff bubbling pots before they order) but the food here is of a high quality, and the beer's good too.

Elegant dishes at Kuchyň

8 U Labutí
MAP B2 ▪ Hradčanské náměstí 11 ▪ 220 511191 ▪ Ⓚ Ⓚ

Restaurant "At the Swans" serves up Zubr lager and some substantial dishes, such as *schnitzel* and goulash. There is seating in the courtyard.

9 Host Restaurant
MAP B2 ▪ Loretánská 15 ▪ 606 123449 ▪ Ⓚ Ⓚ Ⓚ

Stylish dining alongside sweeping views of Petřín Hill and Malá Strana.

10 Lví dvůr
MAP B1 ▪ U Prašného mostu 6
▪ 607 202532 ▪ Ⓚ Ⓚ

This rooftop dining room affords great views of St Vitus Cathedral. Enjoy Lobkowicz Premium beer alongside delicious Czech cuisine.

See map on pp100–101 ←

🔟 Joseof and Northern Old Town

It is impossible to precisely date the arrival of the Jewish community in Prague, but historical sources mention the destruction of a Jewish settlement on the Vltava's left bank in the 13th century. For the next 500 years, Prague's Jewish population was obliged to live in a walled ghetto, where the Josefov quarter is today. Their allotted space was so restricted that they had to bury their dead layer upon layer in the Old Jewish Cemetery. When Emperor Josef II removed these strictures, many of its original residents left the ghetto, which became a slum occupied by the city's poorest population. The quarter was razed in the late 19th century, making way for affluent avenues such as Pařížská. During World War II, the synagogues stored valuables looted from Jewish communities across the Reich. Nearly 80,000 Czech and Moravian Jewish people perished in the Holocaust.

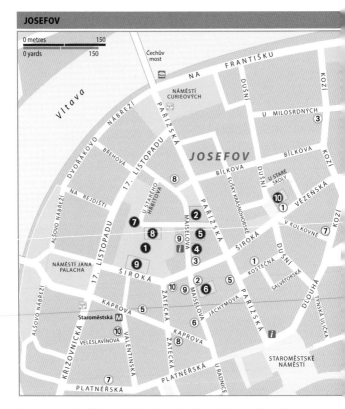

Previous pages Small houses built into the castle walls at Golden Lane, Prague Castle

Headstones, Old Jewish Cemetery

1 Old Jewish Cemetery

The sight of hundreds of graves, their leaning headstones crumbling on top of each other, is a moving and unforgettable experience – a testament to the treatment of the Jewish people in Prague, confined to their own ghetto even in death. Although there is no definite record of the number of burial sites here *(see pp28–9)*, to appreciate the depth of the graveyard, compare the gravestones' height with that of the street level on U Starého hřbitova.

2 Old-New Synagogue

Across the street from the cemetery, Europe's oldest surviving synagogue *(see p44)* has witnessed a turbulent history, including pogroms and fire, and has often been a place of refuge for the city's beleaguered Jewish community. Its name may come from the fact that another synagogue was built after this one, taking the title "new", but which was later destroyed. It is still the religious centre for Prague's small, present-day Jewish community *(see p30)*.

3 St Agnes of Bohemia Convent

This 13th-century Gothic convent *(see pp34–5)* is full of spectacular wall panels and altarpieces, as well as original 13th-century cloisters and chapels. The artworks, part of the gallery's collection, comprise some of the best Czech medieval and early Renaissance art.

- **1** Top 10 Sights
  see pp109–111
- **1** Cafés and Restaurants
  see p113
- **1** Shops
  see p112

Vyšší Brod altarpiece at St Agnes

4 Jewish Town Hall
MAP L3 ■ Maiselova 18
■ Closed to the public

The hands of the Rococo clock on the town hall, or *Židovská radnice*, turn counterclockwise as Hebrew is read from right to left. The building was one of Mordechai Maisel's *(see p43)* gifts to his community in the late 16th century, but it was renovated in Baroque style in 1763.

Jewish Town Hall

5 High Synagogue
MAP L2 ■ Červená 4 ■ Closed to the public

Constructed along with the town hall with funds from Mordechai Maisel, the High Synagogue was built in elegant Renaissance fashion. Subsequent reconstructions updated the exterior, but the interior retains its original stucco vaults. Inside there are also impressive Torah scrolls and mantles.

6 Maisel Synagogue
MAP L3 ■ Maiselova 10 ■ Open Apr–Oct: 9am–6pm Sun–Fri (Nov–Mar: to 4:30pm) ■ Adm

Rudolf II gave Mordechai Maisel permission to build his private synagogue here in the late 16th century, in gratitude for the Jewish mayor's financial help in Bohemia's war against the Turks. At the time of its construction it was the largest synagogue in Prague, until fire destroyed it and much of the ghetto in 1689. It was later rebuilt as a Jewish museum *(see p49)*, in

Neo-Gothic style. Inside is a wonderful collection of Jewish silverwork and other items such as candlesticks and ceramics, much of it looted by the Nazis from synagogues across Bohemia. Ironically, the Third Reich planned to build a museum in Prague, dedicated to the Jewish people as an "extinct race".

7 Ceremonial Hall
MAP K2 ■ U Starého hřbitova 3a ■ Open Apr–Oct: 9am–6pm Sun–Fri (Nov–Mar: to 4:30pm) ■ Adm

Constructed in the early 1900s in striking mock Romanesque fashion, the Ceremonial Hall was home to the Jewish community's Burial Society. The fascinating exhibits housed inside detail the complex Jewish rituals for preparing the dead for the grave.

Early 20th-century Ceremonial Hall

8 Klausen Synagogue
MAP K2 ■ U Starého hřbitova 1
■ Open Apr–Oct: 9am–6pm Sun–Fri (Nov–Mar: to 4:30pm) ■ Adm

Abutting the Old Jewish Cemetery, this Baroque single-nave building was constructed in 1694 on the site of a school and prayer hall *(klausen)* where Rabbi Loew taught the *cabala*. Like most synagogues in the area, it now houses Jewish exhibits *(see p49)*, including prints, pointers and manuscripts.

Torah pointer

RABBI JUDAH LOEW BEN BEZALEL

One of Prague's most famed residents, Rabbi Loew ben Bezalel (c 1520–1609) is associated with numerous local legends but he was also a pioneering pedagogue and a leading Hebrew scholar of the times. Foremost among the myths surrounding Loew is that of the Golem *(see p54)*, a clay automaton the rabbi supposedly created to defend the ghetto.

Vaulted ceilings, Pinkas Synagogue

(9) Pinkas Synagogue
MAP K3 ■ Široká 3 ■ Open Apr–Oct: 9am–6pm Sun–Fri (Nov–Mar: to 4:30pm) ■ Adm

After World War II, this 15th-century Gothic building with some early Renaissance features became a monument to the estimated 80,000 Czech and Moravian victims of the Holocaust – the names and dates of all those known to have died either in the Terezín camp or in others across Eastern Europe are written on the wall in a moving memorial. Equally moving is the exhibition (see p49) of writings and paintings made by the children (of whom there were more than 10,000 under the age of 15) confined in Terezín (see p31).

(10) Spanish Synagogue
MAP M2 ■ Vézeňská 1 ■ Open Apr–Oct: 9am–6pm Sun–Fri (Nov–Mar: to 4:30pm) ■ Adm

The Moorish interior with its swirling arabesques and stucco decoration gives this synagogue (see p45) its name. It stands on the site of the Old School, Prague's first Jewish house of worship. František Škroup, composer of the Czech national anthem, was the organist in the mid-19th century. It hosts exhibitions of Jewish history and synagogue silver.

The Moorish Spanish Synagogue

A DAY IN THE JEWISH QUARTER

▶ MORNING

A sobering place to start the day, the **Pinkas Synagogue** lists Holocaust victims by their home village and name, and helps visitors to appreciate how large the Czech Jewish community once was. Afterwards take a stroll through the adjoining **Old Jewish Cemetery** (see p109), where a guide will help you find significant gravesites. Also worth visiting in this area is the Baroque **Klausen Synagogue**, with its exhibits on Jewish festivals and family life.

A short walk away, at the end of U Starého hřbitova, is the **Old-New Synagogue** (see p109), where you'll find treasures like Rabbi Loew's seat. Exiting, note the **Jewish Town Hall** next door with its Hebrew clock. Inside the Jewish Quarter information centre is **Café Golem** (see p113), a good stop for a light lunch.

AFTERNOON

After lunch, meander among the antiques shops en route to the **Maisel Synagogue**, where you'll find the first part of an exhibit on Jewish settlement in Bohemia and Moravia – it continues at the **Spanish Synagogue** a five-minute walk to the east down Široká.

Refresh yourself at **Bakeshop Praha** (see p112) around the corner before walking a few minutes northeast to the **St Agnes of Bohemia Convent** (see p109) with its exhibits of Czech medieval art.

A truly Josefov-style evening involves a kosher dinner at **King Solomon** (see p113) near the cemetery and a concert of sacred music at the Spanish Synagogue.

See map on pp108–9 ←

Shops

1 Spanish Synagogue Gift Shop
MAP M2 ▪ Vězeňská 1

Exquisite torah pointers, *yarmulkas* (skull caps) and unique gifts, such as a watch in the style of the clock on the Jewish Town Hall *(see p110)*.

2 Kosta Boda
MAP L3 ▪ Maiselova 12

The tiny Josefov outpost of the renowned glassmaker has been producing stunning glass artworks and tablewares since the mid-1700s.

3 Hodinářství (Old Clocks)
MAP L3 ▪ Maiselova 16

If you have trouble finding this small shop selling old clocks, simply stand at the corner of Maiselova and Široká streets and you'll hear the old cuckoo clock sing.

4 Granát Turnov
MAP N2 ▪ Dlouhá 1

Specializing in Bohemian garnet, Granát Turnov is part of Prague's biggest jewellery chain. Jewellery lovers can find a large variety of brooches and necklaces here.

5 Gucci
MAP L3 ▪ Pařížská 9

Treat yourself to high-end luxury fashion from this world-renowned brand. Located on the tree-lined Pařížská street, this store is one of many designer boutiques frequented by tourists and locals alike.

6 Studio Šperk
MAP M2 ▪ Dlouhá 19

Aficionados come to this tiny goldsmith's workshop for eye-catching gold and silver jewellery, much of which is embellished with the celebrated red Bohemian garnet.

The Bakeshop Praha bakery and café

7 Bakeshop Praha
MAP M2 ▪ Kozí 1

Grab a bag of brownies, *rugelach* or butterhorns (small crescent-shaped biscuits) and other mouthwatering treats, or lunch on an egg salad sandwich and coffee. There are also salads and quiches to take away.

8 Antique Kaprova
MAP L3 ▪ Kaprova 12

This serious collector's shop specializes in jewels and small decorative items such as clocks and coins. If you don't find what you're looking for, just ask and they'll point you in the right direction.

9 Antique Cinolter
MAP L3 ▪ Maiselova 9

Art lovers should peruse this small gallery's sale exhibition of local art. The original oils and sketches capture Josefov's bittersweet warmth and humanity.

10 Alma Antique
MAP K3 ▪ Valentinská 7

What don't they sell? Alma Antique is a bazaar stocked with Persian rugs, jewellery, Meissen porcelain, crystal and ornate nesting dolls. This is one of the largest antique dealers in Prague.

Bohemian garnet ring, Studio Šperk

Cafés and Restaurants

1 Krčma
MAP L3 ▪ Kostecná 4 ▪ 725 157262

A medieval-themed tavern just off swanky Pařížská, Krčma offers reasonably priced food, draught beer and lots of low-lit ambiance.

2 Naše maso
MAP N2 ▪ Dlouhá 39 ▪ ⓚⓚ

The casual setting in a butcher shop makes this better suited to a quick bite. The meat is quality local beef and pork. Tell them at the counter how you'd like your meat to be done.

Food for sale at Naše Maso

3 Field
MAP M1 ▪ U Milosrdných 12 ▪ 222 316999 ▪ ⓚⓚⓚ

A stylish restaurant *(see p73)*, with an intimate atmosphere and an interesting mural projected from the ceiling. Innovative dishes and modern cuisine.

4 La Degustation Bohême Bourgeoise
MAP N2 ▪ Haštalská 18 ▪ 222 311234 ▪ ⓚⓚⓚ

La Degustation, a Michelin-starred restaurant *(see p72)*, offers exceptional tasting menus of traditional Czech cuisine, using seasonal ingredients sourced from farmers and foragers.

5 La Bodeguita del Medio
MAP K3 ▪ Kaprova 5 ▪ 224 813922 ▪ ⓚⓚ

This Cuban-Creole restaurant offers grilled fish and meats made using traditional ingredients. Popular with the business crowd, it has a great atmosphere and welcoming staff.

6 Pivnice u Pivrnce
MAP L3 ▪ Maiselova 3 ▪ 777 120382 ▪ ⓚⓚ

A pub with wall decorations by Czech caricaturist Peter Urban. Choose from Czech specialities or enjoy a beer.

7 La Finestra in Cucina
MAP K4 ▪ Platnéřská 13 ▪ 222 325325 ▪ ⓚⓚⓚ

Italian favourites cooked to perfection and great wine are complemented by the fine setting and service *(see p73)*.

8 Les Moules
MAP L2 ▪ Pařížská 19 ▪ www. lesmoules.cz ▪ ⓚⓚ

Enjoy oysters, mussels and other delicious seafood treats at this Belgian restaurant.

9 Café Golem
MAP L3 ▪ Maiselova 15 ▪ 603 962963 ▪ ⓚ

This stylish little café in the Jewish Quarter information centre serves great coffee, bagels, soups and cakes.

10 King Solomon
MAP L3 ▪ Široká 8 ▪ 224 818752 ▪ Closed Fri ▪ ⓚⓚⓚ

Prague's foremost kosher restaurant has separate facilities for meat and dairy dishes. Closes for the sabbath.

Conservatory at King Solomon

See map on pp108–9

🔟 New Town

Founded in 1348, New Town *(Nové Město)* is hardly new. Charles IV's urban development scheme imposed straight avenues on the settlements springing up outside the old city walls and added a fourth town to the constellation of Old Town, Malá Strana and Hradčany. Unlike the Old Town, New Town was a planned grid of streets and markets. The horse market became Wenceslas Square in the 19th century; the 14th-century cattle market, and Europe's largest square, took on Charles's name, becoming Karlovo náměstí. The hay market, Senovážné náměstí, kept its title until the Communists changed it for a time to honour the Russian novelist Maxim Gorky. Since the Velvet Revolution was played out on Národní and Wenceslas Square, these and the surrounding streets have been filled with exciting enterprises.

Lively Wenceslas Square

1 Wenceslas Square

Standing in contrast to the medieval Old Town Square *(see pp18–21)*, the lively Wenceslas Square *(see pp36–7)* expresses the history of 20th-century Prague, from its many beautiful Art Nouveau façades to the memories of the numerous marches, political protests and celebrations that have shaped the city over the past 100 years.

2 Na Příkopě
MAP N5

Formerly a moat protecting the city's eastern flank, Na Příkopě is Prague's fashion boulevard, counting Gant, Benetton, Desigual and Guess among its range of big-name stores. Shoppers jam the pedestrian zone and pavement cafés, streaming between the gleaming Myslbek shopping centre and Slovanský dům, with its 10-screen mulliplex cinema. The Hussite firebrand Jan Želivský preached on the site now occupied by another shopping mall, the Černá Růže Palace.

3 Cathedral of Sts Cyril and Methodius
MAP E5 ▪ Resslova 9 ▪ Open during Holy Masses; opening hours vary

This Baroque church, with a pilastered façade and a small central tower, was built in the 1730s. In the 1930s, the church was given to the Czechoslovak Orthodox Church and dedicated to St Cyril and St Methodius, the 9th-century "Apostles to the Slavs". In 1942, the Heydrich Terror *(see p45)* took place here. A small museum on-site tells the story of these events. In the crypt is the National Memorial to the Heroes of the Heydrich Terror – a bronze plaque has been hung on the wall in their memory.

The Heydrich Terror memorial

④ Franciscan Garden
MAP N6

The Franciscans moved here in 1604, claiming a former Carmelite monastery. The grounds and nearby Church of Our Lady of the Snows had fallen into decay after the Hussite civil war, but the monks beautifully restored them. The area was closed to the public until 1950, when the Communists thought the gardens were worth sharing. Although there's little love lost for the dictatorship of the proletariat, the garden (see p61) remains popular with locals.

The tranquil Franciscan Garden

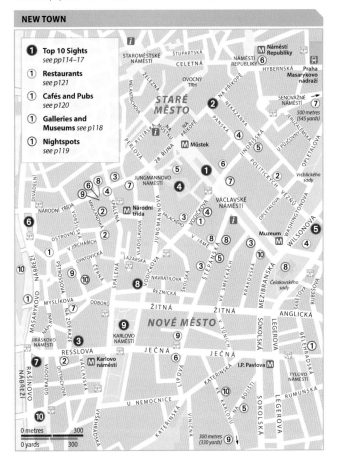

NEW TOWN

① **Top 10 Sights**
see pp114–17

① **Restaurants**
see p121

① **Cafés and Pubs**
see p120

① **Galleries and Museums** see p118

① **Nightspots**
see p119

0 metres 300
0 yards 300

5 State Opera
MAP G4 ▪ Wilsonova 4
▪ www.narodni-divadlo.cz

The first theatre built here, the New Town Theatre, was pulled down in 1885 to make way for the present building (see p66). A Neo-Classical frieze decorates the pediment above the columned loggia at the front of the theatre. The interior is stuccoed, and original paintings in the auditorium and on the curtain have been preserved.

6 National Theatre
MAP E4 ▪ Národní třída 2
▪ www.narodni-divadlo.cz

Patriotic Czechs funded the theatre's construction twice: once in 1868 and again after fire destroyed the build-ing in 1883. To see the stunning allegorical ceiling frescoes and Vojtěch Hynais's celebrated stage curtain, take in one of the operas staged here; good picks are Smetana's *Libuše*, which debuted here, or Dvořák's *The Devil and Kate*. You can see multimedia performances at The New Stage (see p66) next door.

The grand National Theatre

Gehry and Milunic's Dancing House

7 Dancing House
MAP E6 ▪ Jiráskovo náměstí 6
▪ www.galerietancicidum.cz

Built in 1992–6, this edifice by Vlado Milunic and Frank Gehry is known as the Dancing House, or "Ginger and Fred", due to its iconic towers, which resemble two dancers. Most of the building is now a hotel owned by former Czech international football player, Vladimír Šmicer. The two tower rooms, with their castle and Vltava views, are among the best in the capital.

8 New Town Hall
MAP F5 ▪ Karlovo náměstí 1
▪ Tower: open 10am–6pm Tue–Sun
▪ Adm ▪ www.nrpraha.cz

In 1419, an anti-clerical mob led by Jan Želivský hurled the Catholic mayor and his councillors from a New Town Hall window in the first of Prague's defenestrations (see p15). The Gothic tower was added a few years later; its viewing platform is open to the public. Crowds gather at the tower's base most Saturdays to congratulate newlyweds married in the building's Gothic hall.

New Town Hall

MŮSTEK

The area at the bottom of Wenceslas Square takes its name from the "Little Bridge" that spanned the moat here in medieval times. Below the surface, at the top of the escalators descending to the train platform, you'll find the remains of that bridge, uncovered by workers building the metro.

⑨ Karlovo náměstí
MAP F5

Charles IV had his city planners build New Town's central square to the same dimensions as Jerusalem's. Originally a cattle market, it is now a park popular with dog-walkers. Among the trees are monuments to such luminaries as Eliška Krásnohorská, who wrote libretti for Smetana's operas. Many historic buildings line the square today, including the New Town Hall on the square's north side and the Faust House (Faustův dům), which dates back to the 14th century, at its southern end.

Monument at Palackého náměstí

⑩ Palackého náměstí
MAP E6

The riverside square is named for the 19th-century historian František Palacký, whose work was integral to the National Revival. Stanislav Sucharda's sweeping monument to him stands at the plaza's northern end, while the modern steeples of the Emmaus Monastery (see p55) rise from the eastern edge. The church grounds are also known as the Slavonic Monastery, named after the liturgy the resident Balkan Benedictines used. Sadly, American bombs demolished the monastery's original Baroque steeples in 1945 on St Valentine's Day, as part of the Allies' World War II campaign.

A DAY IN NEW TOWN

▶ MORNING

Head to **Wenceslas Square** (see p114) to begin the day's sightseeing. Start with the **National Museum** (see p118) at the top of the square, the nation's leading natural history museum, if only to see the marble stairway, the Pantheon and the city views from the dome. Walk to **St Wenceslas's Statue** and the monument to Communism's victims. Get in a bit of retail therapy as you stroll northwest to Můstek, then visit the **Museum of Communism** (see p118), or enjoy a peaceful stroll through the quiet **Franciscan Garden** (see p115). Then walk 10 minutes west down stately Národní třída towards the river for lunch at **Dynamo** (see p121).

AFTERNOON

A short walk to the river and north along its banks leads you to the **National Theatre** for a glimpse at its magnificent façade. Then follow the Vltava south. Modern-art buffs should stop at **Galerie Mánes** (see p118) on the way. Further south, pause at Jiráskovo náměstí to admire the iconic Post-Modern **Dancing House**. Then turn left and follow Resslova uphill to the **Cathedral of Sts Cyril and Methodius** (see p114) and leafy Karlovo náměstí.

Take in a performance at the National Theatre in the evening; **U Fleků** (see p120) is the obvious choice for dinner, before or after. If you still have the energy, head to **Radost FX** (see p119) to dance the night away or to **Rocky O'Reilly's** (see p119) for its cosy atmosphere and live music.

See map on p115 ←

Galleries and Museums

Galerie Mánes on the Vltava

1 Galerie Mánes
MAP E5 ▪ Masarykovo nábřeží 250 ▪ Opening hours vary ▪ Adm ▪ www.ncvu.eu

Occupying the southern tip of Žofín Island, this contemporary art gallery hosts both Czech and foreign artists.

2 Galerie Via Art
MAP E6 ▪ Resslova 6 ▪ Open 1–5pm Mon–Fri ▪ www.galerieviaart.com

Founded in 1991 as one of Prague's first private galleries, Galerie Via Art exhibits contemporary painting, sculpture and mixed-media art and arranges artist exchanges.

3 Lego Museum
MAP L6 ▪ Národní 31 ▪ Open 10am–8pm daily ▪ https://muzeumlega.cz

This Lego Museum is among the largest in the world. It may essentially be a gift shop with a museum attached, but the impressive Lego sculptures and interactive models will keep the kids entertained.

4 Mucha Museum
MAP P5 ▪ Panská 7 ▪ Open 10am–6pm daily ▪ Adm ▪ www.mucha.cz

Art, Mucha Museum

Art Nouveau artist Alfons Mucha is a celebrated figure in the country. Here you'll find his journals, sketchbooks and paintings, both private and commercial.

5 Museum of Senses
MAP P5 ▪ Jindřišská 20 ▪ Open 9am–8pm daily ▪ www.muzeumsmyslu.cz

This interactive museum (see p58) has over 50 exhibits, including incredible optical illusions.

6 Museum of Communism
MAP P3 ▪ V Celnici 4 ▪ Open 9am–8pm daily ▪ Adm ▪ www.muzeumkomunismu.cz

A triptych of the dream, reality and nightmare that was Communist Czechoslovakia. The museum (see p47) is filled with mementos.

7 Václav Špála Gallery
MAP L6 ▪ Národní 30 ▪ Open 11am–7pm daily ▪ www.galerie vaclavaspaly.cz

This contemporary gallery exhibits works mainly by local artists and aims to make art more accessible.

8 National Museum
MAP G5 ▪ Václavské náměstí 68 ▪ Open 10am–6pm daily ▪ Adm ▪ www.nm.cz

The collection here (see p48) is mainly devoted to archaeology, anthropology, mineralogy, numismatics and natural history.

9 Police Museum
MAP G7 ▪ Ke Karlovu 1 ▪ Open 10am–5pm Tue–Sun ▪ Adm ▪ www.muzeumpolicie.cz

Engaging exhibits, such as an interactive crime scene, document the history of the police.

10 Dvořák Museum
MAP G6 ▪ Ke Karlovu 20 ▪ Open 10am–5pm Tue–Sun ▪ Adm ▪ www.nm.cz

This Baroque palace houses Antonín Dvořák's (see p50) piano and viola, as well as other memorabilia.

Nightspots

① Radost FX
MAP G6 ■ Bělehradská 120

Late at night, club kids take over the disco and lounge *(see p68)*. By day, a broader demographic comes in for the good vegetarian food. Sunday brunch is especially popular. Open until 5am during the weekend.

The bar area at Radost FX

② Balbi Bar
MAP E4 ■ Mikulandská 6

Excellent cocktails, welcoming staff and a cosy atmosphere make this trendy bar the perfect place to spend an evening.

③ Nebe Cocktail & Music Bar
MAP G4 ■ Václavské nám. 56

This bar has over 100 delicious cocktails to choose from. Relax with a drink under the vaulted ceilings, or dance the night away to a mix of current pop and R&B hits, as well as music from the 1980s and 90s.

④ Lucerna Music Bar
MAP N6 ■ Vodičkova 36

The granddaddy of Prague's clubs, the cavernous Lucerna *(see p69)* hosts live jazz as well as rock and dance parties.

⑤ Rocky O'Reilly's
MAP F5 ■ Štěpánská 32

Offering all a Celtophile could ask for, this pub has live music in the evenings, football on the TV, a roaring fire and plenty of stout. The food here is fairly decent as well.

⑥ Reduta Jazz Club
MAP L6 ■ Národní 20

Many celebrated musicians have played here, as has former US President Bill Clinton. Visit to hear all types of jazz from swing bands to modern styles.

⑦ Duplex Club
MAP N6 ■ Václavské nám. 21

During the day, Duplex is an ideal location for lunch or dinner with good views of the city. At night it turns into one of Prague's most exclusive clubs.

⑧ Be Bop Lobby Bar
MAP G4 ■ Štěpánská 40

Set in the luxurious Almanac X hotel *(see p140)*, this Art Deco-style elegant bar offers a wide range of unique signature cocktails, drinks and delicious snacks, along with lively jazz performances in the evening.

⑨ Rock Café
MAP L6 ■ Národní 20

Conveniently set at the heart of the city, Rock Café *(see p69)* hosts live concerts and has a multimedia space that features a theatre and a gallery.

⑩ Zone
MAP E5 ■ Křemencova 10

This atmospheric club in an original stone cellar features stylish lighting and a gracefully curvaceous long bar. A separate lounge is a popular place for various private events.

Partygoers at Zone

See map on p115

Cafés and Pubs

Luxe interiors of the Lucerna Palace

1 Kavárna Lucerna
MAP N6 ▪ Vodičkova 36
▪ 224 215495

Located in the iconic Lucerna Palace (see p36), an architectural gem, this stylish "Lantern" café is the ideal place to enjoy coffee before watching a film or dancing at the nearby club.

2 La Casa de la Havana vieja
MAP E4 ▪ Opatovická 28

A classic Cuban cocktail bar, this captures the vibe of 1930s Cuba, offering a family-friendly atmosphere with modern beverages.

3 Café 35mm
MAP F5 ▪ Štěpánská 35

Students at the Institut Français and other Francophones gather here for coffee, quiche and a quiet read of the French newspapers.

4 Pilsnerka Národní
MAP E4 ▪ Národní 22

This is one of the best places to enjoy Pilsner Urquell. On offer are three types of tapping – milk, šnyt (cut) and hladinka (level).

5 Hostinec U Kalicha
MAP G6 ▪ Na bojišti 12–14

This pub's decor and cartooned walls are based on the Czech novel The Good Soldier Švejk. Author Jaroslav Hašek (see p50) set some of the pivotal scenes here.

6 Pivovarský dům
MAP F6 ▪ Ječná 16
▪ 296 216666

A lovely restaurant and brewery (see p74), with traditional Czech interiors, which offers a unique range of beers.

7 Café Imperial
MAP G2 ▪ Na Poříčí 15
▪ Ⓚ Ⓚ

Enjoy dishes such as braised lamb shank with marjoram and creamed spinach at this popular café.

8 Café Louvre
MAP L6 ▪ Národní 22

Franz Kafka, Max Brod and their writer friends used to hold court here. It's a bright, cheerful place, good for conversation and grabbing a bite to eat. At the back is Prague's classiest pool hall.

9 U Fleků
MAP E5 ▪ Křemencova 11

Exactly what you might expect from the city that created the "Beer-Barrel Polka". U Fleků (see p74) is the city's oldest brewing pub, dating to 1499, and probably the most popular, and the prices reflect it. It is known for its dark lager.

The exterior of U Fleků

10 Oliver's Coffee Cup
MAP G4 ▪ Václavské náměstí 58

Named after the founder's sons, both called Oliver, this cosy café offers a variety of caffeinated drinks, all served by polite and attentive staff.

Restaurants

1 Dynamo
MAP E5 ▪ Pštrossova 29 ▪ 224 932020 ▪ Ⓚ Ⓚ
This Post-Modern diner serves dishes such as rump steak in marinade with thyme and oregano. A wide selection of vegetarian options is on offer.

2 Restaurace Bredovský dvůr
MAP P6 ▪ Politických vězňů 13 ▪ 224 215427 ▪ Ⓚ Ⓚ
Enjoy traditional Czech dishes such as game goulash with Carlsbad dumplings. In the summer, you can eat alfresco.

3 Namaste India Palackého
MAP F4 ▪ Palackého 15 ▪ 776 785786 ▪ Ⓚ Ⓚ
Come here for tasty, traditional Indian cuisine. The restaurant offers an all-you-can-eat buffet.

4 Čestr
MAP G4 ▪ Legerova 75 ▪ 739 266287 ▪ https://cestr.ambi.cz
Meat lovers will get a real kick out of this top-notch smokehouse restaurant, where cuts of beef and pork are cooked to perfection and served along with delicious sides. In addition, you can also sample a range of rare (and expensive) steaks.

5 U Pinkasů
MAP M6 ▪ Jungmannovo náměstí 16 ▪ 221 111152 ▪ Ⓚ Ⓚ
A great-value Czech beer hall since 1843, this is a very popular lunchtime destination. Food is simple but hearty, and the atmosphere lively.

6 Modrý Zub
MAP N6 ▪ Jindřišská 5 ▪ 222 212622 ▪ Ⓚ Ⓚ
This is fast Thai food at its best, great for a quick snack or light meal. Huge windows create a great opportunity for people watching.

PRICE CATEGORIES
For a three-course meal for one with half a bottle of wine (or equivalent meal), taxes and extra charges.
....
Ⓚ under Kč500 Ⓚ Ⓚ Kč500–Kč1,000
Ⓚ Ⓚ Ⓚ over Kč1,000

7 Lemon Leaf
MAP E5 ▪ Myslíkova 14 ▪ 224 919056 ▪ Ⓚ Ⓚ
Thai and Continental specials. The ingredients used are fresh, the presentation colourful and service is fast and friendly.

8 Restaurace Jáma
MAP F4 ▪ V jámě 7 ▪ 222 967081 ▪ Ⓚ Ⓚ
Delicious Tex-Mex and American specialities and a fun atmosphere. Jáma organizes regular parties and sports events.

The interiors of U Šumavy

9 U Šumavy
MAP E5 ▪ Štěpánská 3 ▪ 777 555297 ▪ www.usumavy.cz
This old-fashioned pub restaurant is a little piece of the Czech country-side in central Prague. The food is traditional – everything is served with dumplings.

10 Žofín Garden
MAP E5 ▪ Slovanský ostrov 8 ▪ 775 075066 ▪ www.zofinrestaurant.cz
Near the National Theatre on Slav Island, this restaurant serves elevated takes on traditional Czech game dishes at reasonable prices.

See map on p115

TOP 10 Greater Prague

Prague's city centre can keep most visitors occupied for days, but if you're staying outside the city's heart, or if you have the time to explore beyond the capital's walls, the outlying areas offer plenty of surprises. Over the centuries, the various rulers of Prague have used the surrounding countryside as their personal playground, building impressive castles, palaces and parks to which they could escape the often claustrophobic streets and winding alleyways of the city. Even the Communists have left their own kind of functional mark on the area, with useful edifices, towers and exhibition spaces. From the peaceful parklands of Vyšehrad and the social atmosphere of Letná, to the noisy nightlife of Žižkov and the intriguing gardens of Holešovice and Troja, Greater Prague has a diversity that will fulfil almost any requirements you might have.

Smetana's grave, Vyšehrad

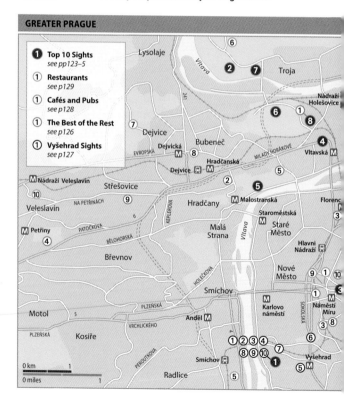

GREATER PRAGUE

- **1** Top 10 Sights
  see pp123–5
- **1** Restaurants
  see p129
- **1** Cafés and Pubs
  see p128
- **1** The Best of the Rest
  see p126
- **1** Vyšehrad Sights
  see p127

1 Vyšehrad
MAP B6 ■ Metro Vyšehrad

The former fortress of Vyšehrad is steeped in legend. Bedřich Smetana paid tribute to the second seat of the Přemyslid dynasty that resided here in the 10th century in his opera *Libuše* and in his rousing work *Má vlast (see p51)*. He is buried here in the National Cemetery, which is also home to the Slavín Monument *(see p127)*.

2 Prague Zoo
MAP B5 ■ U Trojského zámku 3, Troja ■ Opening hours vary, check website ■ Adm ■ www.zoopraha.cz

This zoo *(see p65)* is the second most popular attraction in the country after Prague Castle. Spread across a vast area, it is home to numerous bird and animal species, including elephants, gorillas and giant salamanders.

Church of St Ludmila, Vinohrady

3 Vinohrady
MAP C6

Originally the royal vineyards, Vinohrady today is a gently rolling residential neighbourhood. The central square, Náměstí Míru, features the Neo-Gothic Church of St Ludmila and the Art Nouveau Vinohrady Theatre. For a bit of peace and greenery visit Havlíčkovy sady.

4 Holešovice
MAP B5

Home to the National Gallery's Trade Fair Palace *(see pp32–3)*, which holds the gallery's collection of modern and contemporary art, this once-bustling warehouse district is being redeveloped to make a comeback. Motor car enthusiasts will love the National Technical Museum *(see p49)*, with its exhibits of Czech interwar vehicles such as Škodas, as well as other vintage vehicles.

Cars, National Technical Museum

Statue in Letná Park

5 Letná Park
MAP E1

A grand staircase leads from the Vltava riverbank opposite the Josefov quarter (see pp108–13) to a giant metronome. Prior to this oversized timekeeper, a mammoth statue of Joseph Stalin stood on the plinth here (see p46), but it was blown up in 1962. The surrounding park echoes with the clatter of skateboards and barking dogs. Travelling circuses sometimes set up in the open fields, but Letná's popular beer garden is probably its biggest draw.

6 Stromovka
MAP B5

King Ottokar II established the royal game park here in the 13th century; it's been a public garden since 1804 (stromovka means "place of trees"). Stroll or skate through the ancient park (see p60) by day and visit the planetarium by night. The fish ponds were a creation of Rudolf II – the emperor drilled a tunnel under Letná in the 16th century to bring in water to supply them.

7 Troja Château
MAP B5 ■ U Trojského zámku 1, Troja ■ Open Apr–Nov: 10am–5pm Tue–Thu, Sat & Sun (from 1pm Fri) ■ Adm ■ www.ghmp.cz

One of the most striking summer palaces in Prague, Troja Château was built in the late 17th century by Jean-Baptiste Mathey for Count Sternberg. Surrounded by beautiful gardens and two orangeries, the château has a good collection of 19th-century art and sculpture.

The classical façade of Troja Château

8 Výstaviště
MAP B5

Originally built at the end of the 19th century to host trade shows, this exhibition ground is like nothing else in Prague. Although large parts of the complex are currently being renovated, including the Křižík fountain and the Lapidárium (see p126), the area is still worth a visit on a rainy day for the country's largest aquarium, Mořský Svět. There's also an indoor swimming pool and an ice-hockey rink. The exterior of the Art Nouveau-style Industrial Palace is also a sight to behold.

ŽIŽKOV

This neighbourhood came into existence when city fathers divided the expanding Královské Vinohrady district. The inhabitants of the area thumbed their noses at Habsburg rule and named their new district after the Hussite warrior. Žižkovites' contrary nature runs deep, even having a separatist movement which promotes an independent Republic of Žižkov. An alternative culture thrives around the Akropolis club and the Divus artists collective. Increasingly, the establishment and rising popularity of numerous international restaurants are putting the area on the map.

National Memorial on the Vítkov Hill

9 National Memorial on the Vítkov Hill

MAP C6 ■ Žižkov ■ Open 10am–6pm
Wed–Sun ■ Adm ■ www.nm.cz

The one-eyed Hussite general Jan
Žižka defeated invading crusaders
in 1420 atop the hill where his giant
equestrian statue now stands in front
of the Tomb of the Unknown Soldier.
Erected in 1929, the monument
serves as a memorial to all those
who suffered in the Czech struggle
for independence. The Communists
co-opted the building, and for a time
it served as President Klement
Gottwald's mausoleum (see p46).

10 Žižkov TV Tower

MAP C6 ■ Mahlerovy sady 1
■ Open 9am–midnight ■ Adm ■ www.
towerpark.cz

The Prague TV Tower is the highest
building in Prague, reaching 216 m
(709 ft) in height. However it didn't
begin transmitting until after the
Velvet Revolution (see p43). Three
thematically different "capsules"
at the tower (see p46) offer
unforgettable views of the
city, especially at sunset.
Outside the tower, there
are ten giant sculptures
of babies by Czech
artist David Černý.

Žižkov TV Tower

THREE AFTERNOON WALKS

▶ AFTERNOON ONE

See **Vyšehrad** (see p123) late in
the day, but only if the weather
looks promising. Take the metro
to the Vyšehrad stop at the
Congress Centre (see p127), from
where you have marvellous views
of Prague's spires. Walk west
along Na Bučance and enter the
fortifications through the **Tábor
Gate** (see p127). Once inside the
walls, you'll find historic con-
structions everywhere you turn,
such as the lovely Romanesque
Rotunda of St Martin (see p127).
Enjoy the park at your leisure but
get to the westernmost edge of
the compound atop Vyšehrad's
rocky outcrop in time for sunset.

AFTERNOON TWO

Žižkov and **Vinohrady** (see p123)
are also best seen in the second
half of the day. From Florenc
metro, climb to the **National
Memorial on the Vítkov Hill** for a
wonderful view, then compare it
to the one you get from the **Žižkov
TV Tower**. Take a stroll as far into
Vinohrady as your feet will permit
you, but save your strength: you'll
need it for a night out pubbing
and clubbing.

AFTERNOON THREE

Energetic and keen walkers can
manage to see **Stromovka** and
Troja in half a day. Take the tram
to **Výstaviště**, among the trees of
the former game park, before
crossing the Vltava to the **Troja
Château**. From there, you're
within easy walking distance of
Prague Zoo (see p123). Take
bus 112 back to the metro at
Nádraží Holešovice.

See map on pp122–3 ←

The Best of the Rest

Late 19th-century Lapidárium

1 Lapidárium
MAP B5 ■ Výstaviště 422, Holešovice ■ Closed for renovation ■ Adm ■ www.nm.cz

Several statues including the Marian column from Old Town Square *(see p18)* and sculptures from Charles Bridge *(see p22)* are on display here.

2 National Museum of Agriculture
MAP B5 ■ Kostelní 44, Holešovice ■ Open 9am–5pm Tue–Sun ■ Adm ■ www.nzm.cz

A visit to this museum is an excursion through Czech agricultural history.

3 The City of Prague Museum
MAP H2 ■ Na Poříčí 52 ■ Open 9am–6pm Tue–Sun ■ Adm ■ en.muzeumprahy.cz

Visitors can explore the history of Prague at this museum *(see p48)*.

4 Břevnov Monastery
MAP A6 ■ Markétská 1, Břevnov ■ Check online for tour times ■ Adm ■ www.brevnov.cz

St Adalbert founded this Benedictine monastery in 993. You can see the remains of a Romanesque and an 18th-century church.

5 Bílek Villa
MAP D1 ■ Mickiewiczova 1, Hradčany ■ 233 323631 ■ Open 10am–6pm Tue–Sun ■ Adm ■ www.ghmp.cz

The exhibition of art at this villa captures the essence and style of František Bílek's body of work and techniques.

6 Olšany Cemetery
MAP C6 ■ Vinohradská 153 ■ Open Mar, Apr, Oct: 8am–6pm daily (May–Sep: to 7pm; Nov–Feb: to 5pm)

Many notable Czech personalities, such as Jan Palach *(see p36)* are buried in this vast cemetery. Visitors can get a free map at the entrance.

7 Kafka's Grave
MAP C6 ■ Izraelská 1 ■ Open 9am–5pm Sun–Tue (to 2pm Fri)

Kafka's sombre gravemarker lies close to the entrance along Row 21 at the New Jewish Cemetery.

8 Church of the Most Sacred Heart of Our Lord
MAP C6 ■ Nám. Jiřího z Poděbrad, Vinohrady

Designed by Slovenian architect Josip Plečnik, this modern building was inspired by old Christian architecture.

9 Villa Müller
MAP B6 ■ Nad Hradním vodojemem 14 ■ Adm ■ www.muzeumprahy.cz/en/visit-villa-muller

An avant-garde masterpiece, this villa by Adolf Loos is a fusion of Functionalism and old English-style design. Reservations needed.

DOX Centre for Contemporary Art

10 DOX Centre for Contemporary Art
MAP C5 ■ Poupětova 1, Holešovice ■ Open noon–6pm Wed–Sun ■ Adm ■ www.dox.cz

Set in a former factory, this space *(see p48)* presents contemporary international art, architecture and design.

Vyšehrad Sights

1 Sts Peter and Paul Cathedral

Štulcova ■ Open Apr–Oct: 10am–6pm daily (Nov–Mar: to 5pm) ■ Adm

Although the first church to stand on this site was founded by Vratislav II in the 11th century, the Neo-Gothic structure seen today dates back to 1903. The very valuable Gothic altar with a panel depicting *Our Lady of the Rains* is on the right-hand side of the chapel.

2 Slavín Monument

K Rotundě ■ Open Mar, Apr, Oct: 8am–6pm daily (May–Sep: to 7pm; Nov–Feb: to 5pm)

Set within Vyšehrad Cemetery, this monument marks the burial place of a number of notable Czech cultural figures. Students laid flowers in remembrance here on 17 November 1989, before marching into town for the Velvet Revolution *(see p43)*.

3 Devil's Pillar

K Rotundě

The story goes that the devil bet a local priest that he could carry this pillar from the Church of St Mary in Prague to the boundries of Rome before the clergyman could finish his sermon. Being a sore loser, Satan threw the column he was carrying to the ground here.

4 Tábor Gate (Špička)

V Pevnosti

Charles IV restored Vyšehrad's fortifications in the 14th century. Catholic crusaders rode through this gate on their way to crush the Táborites in 1434.

5 Congress Centre

This ex-Communist palace of culture *(see p46)* now hosts numerous international conferences as well as pop concerts, thanks to its excellent acoustics.

6 Nusle Bridge

This simple, utilitarian viaduct spans the Nusle Valley, connecting New Town to the Pankrác banking and commercial district.

7 Cubist Houses

Czech architect Josef Chochol (1880–1956) built several angular masterpieces in the early 20th century. Take the steps down the hill from Vyšehrad Cemetery to visit the impressive buildings at Rašínovo nábřeží 47, Libušina 49 and Neklanova 98.

8 Smetana's Grave

At the start of each year's Prague Spring International Music Festival *(see p80)*, musicians attend a ceremony at composer Bedřich Smetana's grave.

9 Casemates

V Pevnosti 46 ■ 241 410348 ■ Open 10am–6pm daily ■ Adm

In the 18th century, occupying French troops drilled niches in Vyšehrad rock and built vaults inside to store arms and ammunition. This now houses six original statues from Charles Bridge *(see pp22–3)*.

10 Rotunda of St Martin

K Rotundě

This 11th-century chapel is the oldest in Prague and most likely to be the oldest Christian house of worship in the country. It was reconstructed in 1878.

The simple Rotunda of St Martin

See map on pp122–3

Cafés and Pubs

① Kavárna Pražírna
MAP G6 ▪ Lublaňská
676/50, Vinohrady ▪ 720 385622
▪ www.kavarnaprazirna.cz

Enjoy the flavour and aroma of freshly roasted Arabica coffees at this brick-lined café. Also try the homemade desserts and pickled cheese.

② U Vystřelenýho Oka
MAP C6 ▪ U Božích bojovníků 3, Žižkov ▪ 222 540465 ▪ Closed Sun

The name "At the Shot-Out Eye" is a tribute to the half-blind Hussite general Jan Žižka from whom Žižkov takes its name and whose enormous statue (see p125) looms overhead.

U Vystřelenýho Oka sign

③ U Holanů
MAP H7 ▪ Londýnská 10, Vinohrady

Tuck into a plate of pickled sausages or herring at Vinohrady's favourite no-nonsense pub. Simple but clean, with perfunctory service; they don't make them like this anymore.

④ U Houdků
MAP C6 ▪ Bořivojova 110, Žižkov ▪ 222 711239

This hidden little gem in Žižkov serves Czech meals that are great value for money. In summer you can sit outside.

⑤ Palác Akropolis
MAP C6 ▪ Kubelíkova 27, Žižkov ▪ www.palacakropolis.com

One of the most active independent cultural centres in Prague, Akropolis (see p68) annually hosts nearly a 1,000 cultural events. Both local as well as top international artists perform here.

⑥ Mecca
MAP C5 ▪ U Průhonu 3, Holešovice ▪ www.mecca.cz

With emphasis on good service, Mecca (see p69) has become a synonym for dance music from around the world and is known for its international acts. It has five super-fast bars and two music stages.

⑦ Dva Kohouti
MAP B5 ▪ Sokolovská 55, Karlín ▪ 604 611001 ▪ www.dvakohouti.cz

With dozens of beers on tap, this brewery with a pub is a hugely popular Karlín hangout. Try the exceptional homebrewed pilsner.

⑧ Hlučná samota
MAP H7
▪ Zahřebská 14, Vinohrady

This refined pub takes its name from Bohumil Hrabal's 1976 short novel *Too Loud a Solitude* (see p51). Neither loud nor solitary, this pub offers its guests excellent food and beer, for which they loyally return every time.

⑨ Můj šálek kávy
MAP B5 ▪ Křižíkova 105, Karlín ▪ 725 556944 ▪ www.mujsalekkavy.cz

Sip away at speciality coffee and savour homemade cakes and cookies at the flagship café of Czech double-shot coffee roasters. The interesting decor includes bare walls, books and artwork.

⑩ Pastička
MAP B6 ▪ Blanická 25, Vinohrady

The Mousetrap is a perfect blend of old-fashioned beer hall and modish gastropub. Visit it for a choice of light and semi-dark Bernard beer, good, filling food and eclectic Irish decor.

Modern decor at Pastička gastropub

Restaurants

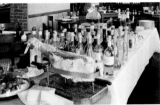

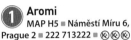

The dining room at Aromi

PRICE CATEGORIES

For a three-course meal for one with half a bottle of wine (or equivalent meal), taxes and extra charges.

Ⓚ under Kč500 ⓀⓀ Kč500–Kč1,000 ⓀⓀⓀ over Kč1,000

1 Aromi

MAP H5 ▪ Náměstí Míru 6, Prague 2 ▪ 222 713222 ▪ ⓀⓀⓀ

This excellent Italian restaurant serves up a fantastic menu of traditional food accompanied by an extensive range of wines from all around the world.

2 Olympos

MAP C6 ▪ Kubelíkova 9, Žižkov ▪ 222 722239 ▪ ⓀⓀ

Prague's best Greek food is on offer here. The large garden, complete with a children's playground, is ideal for summer dining. The mixed salad platter is the best value around.

3 Mailsi

MAP C6 ▪ Lipanská 1, Žižkov ▪ 774 972010 ▪ ⓀⓀ

This little Pakistani food spot offers better value than the Indian restaurants in the centre. Located close to the No. 9 tram stop, it's not as remote as it appears.

4 SaSaZu

MAP C5 ▪ Bubenské nábřeží 306, Holešovic ▪ 284 097455 ▪ www.sasazu.com

This Holešovice landmark offers a menu of exceptional dishes inspired by Asian street food. At night, it also becomes a popular live music venue *(see p68)*.

5 Na Kopci

MAP B6 ▪ K Závěrce 20, Praha 5 ▪ 251 553102 ▪ ⓀⓀ

Featured in the Michelin guide as a "Bib Gourmand" restaurant, Na Kopci offers an excellent four-course degustation menu of French and Czech delicacies created with seasonal and local ingredients.

6 Salabka

MAP B5 ▪ K Bohnicím 2, Praha 7 ▪ 778 019002 ▪ Closed Sun–Tue ▪ ⓀⓀⓀ

Surrounded by vast vineyards, this restaurant located near the district of Troja, is renowned for its award-winning wines. The menu here follows the latest trends with wild game and offers local freshwater fish dishes.

7 Chorvatský Mlýn

MAP A5 ▪ Horoměřická 3a, Praha 6, Dejvice ▪ 220 610760 ▪ ⓀⓀ

Standing on the site of the original 17th-century mill, "Croatian Mill" is located in the centre of the Divoká Šárka Nature Reserve. It serves sumptuous Mediterranean cuisine.

8 U Cedru

MAP B5 ▪ Národní Obrany 27, Dejvice ▪ 233 342974 ▪ ⓀⓀ

For a traditional Lebanese dining experience, order pitta with hummus, tabbouleh and other appetizers.

9 LA VIE Mánesova

MAP C6 ▪ Mánesova 13, Vinohrady ▪ 728 274260 ▪ ⓀⓀⓀ

This restaurant, with a beautiful decor, serves steaks, stuffed beef and soups prepared with fresh ingredients.

10 U Marčanů

MAP A6 ▪ Veleslavínská 14, Prague 6 ▪ 235 360623 ▪ Ⓚ

Folk music and dancing make this a fun lunch spot. Large portions of Czech food are served at communal tables. Book ahead and take a taxi.

See map on pp122–3

Streetsmart

Colourful old buildings in the historic
Prague quarter of Malá Strana

Getting Around

Arriving by Air

Václav Havel Airport Prague (PRG), 16 km (10 miles) northwest of the city centre, is Prague's only international airport. Terminal 2 serves the Schengen zone: mainly continental EU countries and Switzerland. Terminal 1 serves other destinations, including the UK and Ireland. The airport is well served by international airlines, with direct connections to major European cities, plus many Middle Eastern cities. There are normally no direct flights to North America, although **Czech Airlines** (ČSA) and **Delta** sometimes offer flights to New York (JFK) or Atlanta over Christmas and summer holidays.

Both the terminals are modern, well-maintained structures, with shops, restaurants, ATMs, car rental offices and tourist information booths.

Getting to and from Prague airport is easy, economical and relatively fast. The two terminals are connected to the town centre through buses, minibuses and taxis. Prague Public Transit bus No 119 runs regularly from 4:30am to midnight and departs from just outside the arrivals area of both terminals. Take it to the line's last station, Nádraží Veleslavín, then switch to metro line A into the city centre. Tickets (Kč40, good for both the bus and metro) can be bought at public transport booths inside the terminals, or from orange ticket vending machines (have local currency handy). Another option is the Airport Express bus to the main railway station (100Kč – tickets from the driver). There are shared shuttle minibuses, run by **Prague Airport Shuttles**, which leave for the city centre every 15 minutes; expect to pay between Kč165 and Kč450, depending on numbers. You can also request to be dropped off at your hotel or accommodation. Taxis line up outside the arrival halls of both terminals and cost about Kč700 to the centre.

International Train Travel

Regular high-speed international trains connect Prague's Hlavní nádraží and Nádraží Holešovice stations to major cities in Europe. Reservations for these services are essential as seats book up quickly, particularly in the busy summer months.

You can buy tickets and passes for multiple international journeys from **Eurail** or **Interrail**, however you may still need to pay an additional reservation fee depending on what rail service you travel with. Always check that your pass is valid on the service on which you wish to travel before boarding. Students and those under the age of 26 can benefit from discounted rail travel. For more information on discounted rail travel both in and to the Czech Republic, visit the Interrail or Eurail website.

Domestic Train Travel

The railways in the Czech Republic are run by **České Dráhy (ČD)**.

The biggest and busiest railway station in Prague is Hlavní nádraží, which is only a 5-minute walk from Wenceslas Square. After a thorough renovation, the Art Nouveau station now features a gleaming interior with shops, restaurants, a pub and even a jeweller. The lower ground floor has an inexpensive left-luggage facility and the central ticket office (open 3:20–12:30am). There is also a ČD Travel office, where all international rail tickets are available from multilingual station staff and ticket machines.

There are several types of train services operating in Prague and throughout the Czech Republic, including the *rychlík* (express) trains; the *osobní* (passenger) trains which form a local service and stop at all stations; and the express, for longer distances.

Tickets can be bought in advance. If you want to buy a ticket just before your train leaves, be aware that queues at ticket booths can be long.

On the timetable, an "R" in a box by a train number means you must have a seat reserved on that train. An "R" without a box means a reservation is recommended. If you are caught in the wrong carriage, you will have to pay an on-the-spot fine.

Public Transport

Prague's bus, tram and metro services are provided by the Prague Public Transport Company (**DPP**). Its website and app provide timetables, ticket information, transport maps and more.

The best way of getting around central Prague by public transport is by tram or metro. Prague's rush hours are between 6am and 9am and 3pm and 5pm, Monday to Friday. However, more trains, trams and buses run at these times, so crowding is not usually a problem. Some bus routes to the suburbs only run during peak hours. It is worth noting that the city centre is compact, and so most of the major sights are within walking distance of one another.

Tickets

Prague has a fully integrated public transport system. As such, tickets are conveniently valid on all forms of public transport in the city, including bus, tram, metro, rail and boat services, and even the funicular railway that runs from Újezd to the top of Petřín Hill.

Tickets are available from machines at metro stations, main tram stops and at most news stands (tabák) which can be found at various locations throughout the city.

Buy tickets before you travel and validate them in the machines provided. Periodic checks are carried out by plain-clothes ticket inspectors who will levy a large on-the-spot fine if you are caught without a valid ticket. Children under 6 travel free and tickets for children aged 6–15 are half price.

Individual ticket prices add up; longer-term tickets are good value if you are planning on exploring the city thoroughly. Network tickets offer unlimited travel for a set number of days. Tickets are available for one day (Kč120) and three days (Kč330).

You can buy paperless public transport tickets direct from your mobile or smart device using the PID Lítačka app.

Buses

Visitors are likely to use a bus only to travel to and from the airport, or to sights further out of town, such as the zoo. There are three bus lines that operate in Malá Strana, Old Town and New Town.

Bus timetables are located at every stop. Daytime buses run from 5am to midnight every 6–30 minutes. Night buses (routes 901–915) operate from midnight to 4:30am every 20–60 minutes.

Usual fares apply. Tickets bought on board are more expensive and can be paid for in cash only. Validate your pre-bought tickets in the machine located at each door.

Long-Distance Bus Travel

Long-distance bus or coach travel can be a cheap option for those visiting Prague and some Czech towns, such as Karlovy Vary, Hradec Králové, Český Krumlov and Terezín, are much easier to reach by coach than train.

The city's main bus terminal is Florenc, on the northeastern edge of the New Town.

Flixbus and **RegioJet** offer a variety of routes to Prague from other European cities as well as several domestic routes. Fares are very reasonable and there are discounts for students, children and seniors.

Trams

Trams are Prague's oldest and most efficient method of public transport. The city's comprehensive tram network covers quite a large area, including the city centre.

Maps and timetables at tram stops help you locate your destination and route. On the timetable, the stop you are at will be underlined and stops below the line will indicate where the tram is heading. The direction of travel is given by the terminus station.

Routes 9, 14, 17 and 22 are the most useful for getting around the centre of Prague. They pass many of the major sights on both sides of the Vltava, and are a cheap and pleasant way of sightseeing.

Trams run 4:30am–12:30am daily every 4–20 minutes. Night trams (routes 91–99) run every 30 minutes and are marked by white numbers on a dark background at stops.

Tram tickets are also valid for travel on the metro and buses, but they must be bought before travel. Validate your ticket using the yellow machines on board.

Metro

The metro is the fastest way to get around the city. Prague's underground system has four lines (A, B, C and D) operating from 5am until midnight every 1–4 minutes at peak times during weekdays (6–9am and 3–5pm daily), and every 4–10 minutes during off-peak times.

Line A (green) is the most useful metro line for tourists, covering all the main areas of the city centre – Prague Castle, the Old Town, Malá Strana and the New Town – including the main shopping area around Wenceslas Square.

Stations are signposted in both English and Czech, and feature information panels in a number of languages.

Taxis

All taxis in Prague are privately owned, and there are many unscrupulous drivers who are out to charge as much as they can get away with. If you think you have been scammed by a taxi driver, take their name and number so you can report them to the police.

Look for Fair Place taxi ranks marked with a yellow "taxi" sign and an orange "thumbs up" icon. Taxis that stop here will guarantee the maximum charges of Kč40 boarding fee, Kč28 per km travel and Kč6 per minute waiting. After the journey, the driver is obliged to print an official receipt.

Taxi companies that are safe to hail on the street include **AAA Taxi**. However, the cheapest way to get a taxi is to phone or use the company's mobile app.

Unless your Czech pronunciation is very good, it is useful to have your destination written down in Czech.

Driving to Prague

The Czech Republic is easily reached by car from most countries in Europe via E-roads, the International European Road Network.

Prague is connected to every major border crossing by motorways (D roads) and expressways (R roads). To drive on the motorway you will need to display a special highway toll sticker available at the border, petrol stations and post offices.

Car Rental

To rent a car in the Czech Republic, you must be at least 21 years old and have held a valid licence for at least one year. Drivers under the age of 26 may incur a young driver surcharge.

EU driving licences issued by any of the EU member states are valid throughout the European Union. If visiting from outside the EU, you may need to apply for an International Driving Permit (IDP). Check with your local automobile association before you travel.

Driving in Prague

Driving in Prague is not recommended. The city's complex web of one-way streets, lack of parking and pedestrianized areas make driving very difficult.

Beware of cyclists and trams in the city. Trams take precedence; take care when turning; and allow cyclists priority.

Vehicles must be parked on the right hand side of the road, with the exception of one-way streets.

Parking spaces in the centre are scarce, and the penalties for illegal parking are harsh. **Parkuj v klidu** provide detailed information regarding parking. Meter parking from 8am to 8pm costs a maximum Kč80 per hour. Orange zones allow parking for two hours and violet zones for a maximum of 24; blue zones are reserved for residents. To use the meter, insert coins for the amount of time you need. The inspection is done automatically by the monitoring system based on the registration mark (licence plate) of the vehicle. Unfortunately, car theft is rife. Try to park in an official – preferably underground – car park or at one of the guarded car parks (look for the "P+R" symbol) at the edge of the city and use public transport to travel in.

If a car accident occurs, the vehicle cannot be moved until there has been a police inspection. In case of emergency, you can call the road traffic assistance, Autoklub Bohemia Assistance (ÚAMK), on the phone number 1240.

Rules of the Road

Always drive on the right. Unless signposted otherwise, vehicles coming from the right have right of way.

At all times, drivers must carry a valid driver's licence, registration and insurance documents.

The law states that both driver and all passengers should wear seat belts. Small children must travel in the back seat.

The use of a mobile phone while driving is strictly prohibited, with the exception of a hands-free system.

Speed limits and a zero tolerance drink-driving policy are strictly enforced in Prague.

Cycling

Prague is generally a bike-friendly city, with many designated cycle lanes.

Ride on the right. Beware of tram tracks; cross them at an angle to avoid getting stuck. For your own safety, do not walk with your bike in a bike lane or cycle on pavements, in pedestrian zones, or in the dark without lights. Wearing a helmet is recommended.

Bicycles can be rented hourly or by the day. Deposits are usually paid upfront and refunded on return. **Praha Bike** offers private rentals and tours. Public bicycle schemes such as **Rekola**, which is operated through an app, are also available.

As part of the **Prague–Vienna Greenways Project**, well-maintained bike paths line both sides of the Vltava, and there are a number of biking trails linking Prague and Vienna. Details of other bike tours and excursions are available from Prague City Tourism *(see p138)*.

Prague by Boat

Regular transport tickets are also valid on the public boat service (lines P1–6).

Boat tours along the Vltava river allow for fabulous views of Prague's major sights. Most run during the summer months, and include one- or two-hour tours, romantic dinner cruises and private rentals.

Tickets can be booked in advance from tour providers. Check out **Evropská Vodní Doprava** or **Prague Boats**. Alternatively you can enquire

on the day at one of the many boarding points along the river.

Walking

Walking is the best – and often the only – way to see much of the city. The centre is about 4 km (2.5 miles) from end to end and many of the historic sights are in pedestrian zones. Wear flat-soled comfortable shoes, watch your step on the cobblestones, and keep a look out for trams that have priority of crossing.

Guided walking tours abound, with themes that include historic Prague and haunted Prague. Most tours meet up just below the Astronomical Clock on Old Town Square.

DIRECTORY

TAXIS

AAA Taxi
w aaataxi.cz

DRIVING IN PRAGUE

Parkuj v klidu
w parkujvklidu.cz

ÚAMK
w uamk.cz

CYCLING

Prague–Vienna Greenways Project
w praguevienna greenways.org

Praha Bike
w prahabike.cz

Rekola
w rekola.cz

PRAGUE BY BOAT

Prague Boats
w prague-boats.cz

Evropská Vodní Doprava
w evd.cz

Practical Information

Passports and Visas

For entry requirements, including visas, consult your nearest Czech embassy or check the **Ministry of Foreign Affairs of the Czech Republic** website. From late 2023, citizens of the UK, US, Canada, Australia and New Zealand do not need a visa for stays of up to three months, but must apply in advance for the European Travel Information and Authorization System (**ETIAS**). Visitors from other countries may also require an ETIAS, so check before travelling. EU nationals do not need a visa or an ETIAS.

Government Advice

It is important to seek both your and the Czech government's advice before travelling. The **UK Foreign, Commonwealth & Development Office (FCDO)**, the **US State Department**, the **Australian Department of Foreign Affairs and Trade** and the **Ministry of the Interior of the Czech Republic** offer the latest information on security, health and local laws.

Customs Information

You can find information on the laws relating to goods and currency taken in or out of the Czech Republic on the **Customs Administration of the Czech Republic** website.

For EU citizens there are no duties on reasonable quantities of most goods meant for personal use carried in or out of the Czech Republic. Exceptions include firearms, weapons and certain foods, plants and endangered species. If travelling outside the EU, limits vary so check restrictions before departing. If you take regular medicine, bring adequate supplies and carry your prescription with you.

Insurance

We recommend that you take out a comprehensive insurance policy covering theft, loss of belongings, medical care, cancellations and delays, and read the small print carefully. The Czech Republic has reciprocal health agreements with other EU countries. EU residents will receive state-provided emergency treatment if they have a valid European Health Insurance Card (EHIC) or UK Global Health Insurance Card (**GHIC**), but note that dental care is not covered. Non-EU visitors should check if their country has reciprocal arrangements with the Czech Republic.

Health

There is a good standard of health care in the Czech Republic and Czech dental care is considered to be among the best in Europe.

If you have an EHIC or GHIC, be sure to present this as soon as possible. You may have to pay after treatment and reclaim the money later.

For other visitors, payment of medical expenses is the patient's responsibility. It is therefore important to arrange comprehensive medical insurance beforehand. For minor ailments and prescriptions go to a pharmacy (lékárna). These are easily identified by a large green cross. Most operate during normal working hours, from 8am to 6pm Monday to Friday. Details of the nearest 24-hour service are usually displayed in pharmacy windows.

There are no vaccinations required for visiting the Czech Republic. Unless stated otherwise, tap water is safe to drink.

Smoking, Alcohol and Drugs

Prague has a strict smoking ban in all public spaces including buildings, bars, cafés, shops, restaurants and hotels.

The possession of narcotics is prohibited. Possession of illegal substances could result in prosecution and a prison sentence.

There is no blanket ban on the consumption of alcohol on the streets; however, drinking alcohol on the bus or train and in metro stations, parks, playgrounds and near schools is banned and may incur a fine. Many Old Town streets have banned walking around with an open bottle or can.

The Czech Republic enforces a strict zero tolerance policy on drink-driving. This also applies to cyclists.

ID

It is compulsory for visitors to carry a form of ID at all times, or failing that, a photocopy of your passport.

Personal Security

Prague is relatively safe and street violence is rare. Pickpocketing is common, particularly on crowded trams, on the metro and at popular tourist sites. Use your common sense and be alert to your surroundings. Avoid hailing taxis on the street; instead, call or ask someone to call for a reliable radio taxi (see p134).

If you have anything stolen, report the crime as soon as possible to the nearest police station, and bring ID with you. Get a copy of the crime report in order to claim on your insurance.

If you have your passport stolen, or if you are involved in a serious crime or accident, contact your embassy as soon as possible.

The ambulance, police and fire brigade can be reached on the Europe-wide **emergency** number 112. The operators speak English and calls are free. There are also dedicated lines for the **ambulance**, **fire brigade** and **police**.

Generally, Czechs are accepting of all people, regardless of their race, gender or sexuality. Homosexuality was legalized in 1962. If you do feel unsafe, the **Safe Space Alliance** pinpoints your nearest place of refuge.

Travellers with Specific Requirements

Narrow streets and uneven paving make Prague difficult for wheelchair users. However, services are improving. Most public buildings are now fitted with entry ramps. Most of the trams and buses have low access, and the majority of metro stations are fitted with lifts. Timetables at tram stops indicate which services are wheelchair-accessible. Visit the Prague Public Transport Company (**DPP**) website to plan your journey using wheelchair-accessible metro stations, trams and buses.

Airport assistance is available for free but must be booked in advance through your airline or travel agency. **Accessible Prague** can arrange transport from the airport to the city centre for wheelchair users. They can also help with finding suitable accommodation and they organize tours and day trips tailored to visitors' needs.

Another useful source of information is the **Prague Organization of Wheelchair Users**, which has a range of resources available, including maps and guides in Braille.

DIRECTORY

PASSPORTS AND VISAS

ETIAS
w etiasvisa.com

Ministry of Foreign Affairs of the Czech Republic
w mzv.cz

GOVERNMENT ADVICE

Australian Department of Foreign Affairs and Trade
w smartraveller.gov.au

Ministry of the Interior of the Czech Republic
w mvcr.cz

UK Foreign, Commonwealth & Development Office (FCDO)
w gov.uk

US Department of State
w travel.state.gov

CUSTOMS INFORMATION

Customs Administration of the Czech Republic
w celnisprava.cz

INSURANCE

GHIC
w gov.uk/global-health-insurance-card

PERSONAL SECURITY

Ambulance
(155

Emergency
(112

Fire Brigade
(150

Police
(158

Safe Space Alliance
w safespacealliance.com

TRAVELLERS WITH SPECIFIC REQUIREMENTS

Accessible Prague
w accessibleprague.com

Prague Organization of Wheelchair Users
w presbariery.cz

DPP
w dpp.cz/en/barrier-free-travel

Time Zone

The Czech Republic is on Central European Time (CET). It is 11 hours behind Australian Eastern Standard Time (AEST), six hours ahead of US Eastern Standard Time (EST) and an hour ahead of Greenwich Mean Time (GMT). The clock moves forward one hour during daylight saving time (last Sunday in March until the last Sunday in October).

Money

The Czech Republic's currency is the koruna or crown (Kč). Most establishments accept major credit, debit and prepaid currency cards. Contactless payments are becoming increasingly common, but it's always a good idea to carry some cash for smaller items and local markets.

Tipping in restaurants is considered polite and a 10 per cent tip of the total bill is appreciated. In hotels, porters generally expect Kč50 per bag, housekeeping Kč30 per day and the concierge Kč30–50 per day. Taxi drivers don't expect a tip.

Electrical Appliances

The electricity supply is 220–240V AC. Plugs come with two round pins, the standard plug type used across much of Continental Europe. Depending on the appliance, you'll need an adaptor and possibly also a converter. Many modern electronics, like laptops and mobiles, have a built-in transformer and only require an adaptor.

Mobile Phones and Wi-Fi

Free Wi-Fi hotspots are widely available in Prague's city centre. Cafés and restaurants usually permit the use of their Wi-Fi on the condition that you make a purchase.

Visitors travelling to Prague with EU tariffs can use their devices abroad without being affected by data roaming charges. Users will be charged the same rates for data, SMS and voice calls as they would pay at home.

Postal Services

Stamps can be bought from post offices, newsagents and tobacconists (tabák).

Parcels and registered letters must be sent from a post office. There is no first- or second-class mail, but the majority of letters usually arrive at their destination within a few days.

The **Main Post Office** (Hlavní pošta), located at Jindřišská 14, is lovely inside and worth a visit, whether or not you need to mail a postcard, letter or parcel.

Weather

The weather in Prague is unpredictable, and given the northern European climate, an umbrella or raincoat will be handy all year around. The best times to visit are spring and autumn, without the summer crowds and with relatively reliable weather. Winter is comparatively quiet, although the benefits of having the city to yourself are offset by daytime highs just above freezing and sunsets at 5pm. Depending on the year, summer can be hot and muggy or cool and rainy. Even in midsummer it's wise to pack a sweater for the evenings.

Opening Hours

Shops in the city centre generally open from 9am to 6pm Monday to Saturday. Malls and shopping centres stay open until 8pm or 9pm. Some shops close early on Saturdays and close for the day on Sundays.

Various museums and attractions are closed on Mondays. Last admission to many attractions is 30 minutes before closing.

On public holidays, schools, banks and most public services are closed and some museums, attractions and shops close early or for the day.

The COVID-19 pandemic proved that situations can change suddenly. Always check before visiting attractions and hospitality venues for up-to-date hours and booking requirements.

Visitor Information

Prague City Tourism is the city's official tourist-information service. It has offices at the airport, and one on the Old Town Square. There's another at the bottom of Wenceslas Square (on the corner of Na Můstku and Rytířská streets).

English-speaking staff offer brochures, maps and information on what's on, where to eat, where to stay and transport. Their official website is useful and well laid out.

The popular **Expats.cz** features event and film listings, articles about life in Prague and restaurant reviews. The **Taste of Prague** blog is by a Czech couple, both avowed foodies, on what to eat and where to eat it; they also run food tours. **Pivní Deníček**, a website and app, shows the nearest bar to your location, which beer they serve on tap and how much it costs.

There are a number of passes or discount cards available for visitors to the city. These can be purchased online or from participating tourist offices. Most offer free or discounted access to Prague's top sights, including exhibitions, museums and tours. Some even cover transport costs. The cards are not free, so consider carefully how many of the offers you are likely to take advantage of before purchasing to ensure you get a good deal.

The **Prague CoolPass** includes entry to 70+ attractions and discounted entry to many more sites, tours, cruises and concerts. The pass is available for one (€50), two (€76), three (€87), four (€94), five (€103) or six (€112) days. You can download a digital pass via a mobile app or receive a physical card from participating tourist offices.

Valid for 30 days from first use, the **Prague City Pass** includes discounted entry to Prague's most popular attractions and tours. The card costs Kč1390.

Local Customs

The Czechs are fiercely proud of their language and its difficult pronunciation, often finding foreigners' attempts at speaking it amusing.

It is an offense to drop litter on the streets. If caught, you will be given a hefty on-the-spot fine.

Language

The Slavic language of Czech is the official language of the Czech Republic. English replaced Russian as the second language of choice after the Velvet Revolution (1989). Those working in the tourist industry usually have a good level of English, French, Russian and often German too, but it's appreciated if you know a few phrases in Czech.

Taxes and Refunds

VAT in the Czech Republic is usually around 20 per cent for most items. Non-EU residents are entitled to a tax refund on single purchases exceeding Kč2000, subject to certain conditions. This does not include tobacco or alcohol.

When you make a purchase, ask the sales assistant for a tax-free cheque. When leaving the country, present this form, along with the goods receipt and your ID at customs.

Accommodation

Prague offers a huge variety of accommodation, comprising luxury five-star hotels, family-run B&Bs, budget hostels and self-catering apartments.

Prices are often inflated during peak season (spring, early and late summer, Easter and Christmas holidays), so it's worth booking well in advance. Prague City Tourism provides a list of accommodation to suit all needs.

You can save a considerable amount on your hotel bill by exploring accommodation options outside the central areas. The neighbourhoods of Holešovice, Žižkov, Karlín, and Smíchov, for example, all have good connections to the centre and a variety of places to stay.

DIRECTORY

POSTAL SERVICES

Main Post Office
ⓦ ceskaposta.cz

VISITOR INFORMATION

Expats.cz
ⓦ expats.cz

Pivní Deníček
ⓦ pivnidenicek.cz

Prague City Pass
ⓦ praguecity
pass.com

Prague City Tourism
ⓦ prague.eu

Prague CoolPass
ⓦ praguecool
pass.com

Taste of Prague
ⓦ tasteofprague.com

Places to Stay

PRICE CATEGORIES
For a standard, double room per night (with breakfast if included), taxes and extra charges.

Ⓚ under Kč3,000 ⒦Ⓚ Kč3,000–6,000
ⓀⓀⓀ over Kč6,000

Luxury Hotels

Archibald At the Charles Bridge
MAP D3 ▪ Na Kampě 15 ▪ 257 531430 ▪ www. archibaldatthecharles bridge.cz ▪ ⓀⓀ
Also known by its address Na Kampě 15, the hotel is close enough to the river that the guests here can hear the Vltava rushing over the weir and the cries of the gulls. The rooms and suites are warmly furnished in a country style.

Hotel Hoffmeister
MAP D1 ▪ Pod Bruskou 7 ▪ 251 017111 ▪ www. hoffmeister.cz ▪ ⓀⓀ
The Hoffmeister is a quiet, modern hotel in the shadow of Prague Castle, celebrated for its gourmet restaurant and gallery of caricatures by the owner's father. The airy rooms are sumptuously and uniquely furnished, and there are lovely outdoor spaces. There is an excellent spa.

Hotel Pod věží
MAP D3 ▪ Mostecká 2 ▪ 257 532041 ▪ www. podvezi.com ▪ ⓀⓀ
The "Hotel Under the Tower" guards the Malá Strana end of Charles Bridge. Rooms are graciously outfitted with period furniture and comfortable reproductions. For a bite to eat visit Café Creperie, which is located downstairs.

The King Charles
MAP B2 ▪ Úvoz 4 ▪ 234 614813 ▪ www.axxos hotels.com/the-king-charles ▪ ⓀⓀ
The two town houses in which the King Charles Hotel is set were created in 1639 from a Gothic Benedictine building. The hotel was popular in the 17th century for the healing powers of its well. The decor is a blissful marriage of Baroque furnishings and modern luxuries.

Almanac X Prague
MAP G4 ▪ Štepánská 40 ▪ 222 820000 ▪ www. almanachotels.com/ praguex ▪ ⓀⓀⓀ
In the 1930s the Alcron, now the Almanac X, was Prague's answer to the Ritz in New York. This historic hotel with period furnishings and high ceilings has had its Art Deco dandiness – besmirched by 40 years of secret police surveillance – revived. The hotel is undergoing renovation work, so while most of the bedrooms and its famous Be Bop Bar (see p119) are open, the restaurant and rooftop bar are due to reopen later in 2023 and 2024.

Four Seasons
MAP K3 ▪ Veleslavínova 2a ▪ 221 427000 ▪ www. fourseasons.com/prague ▪ ⓀⓀⓀ
Swaddled in the classic Four Seasons trademark luxury, guests may well forget where they are. A quick stroll on the hotel's riverside terrace should remind them. The CottoCrudo restaurant is among Prague's best.

Golden Well Hotel
MAP C2 ▪ U Zlaté studně 4 ▪ 257 011213 ▪ www. goldenwell.cz ▪ ⓀⓀⓀ
Once belonging to the astronomer Tycho Brahe, Golden Well Hotel sits in Malá Strana's twisting maze of streets, adjoining the Ledeburg Gardens and offering unparalleled views. Rooms have whirlpool baths and Richelieu furniture. The terrace restaurant (see p73) is one of Prague's top choices.

Grand Hotel Bohemia
MAP P3 ▪ Králodvorská 4 ▪ 234 608111 ▪ www. grandhotelbohemia.cz ▪ ⓀⓀⓀ
Old European decorum meets Old European decadence: built in 1920s, the Bohemia housed one of the liveliest clubs in Jazz Age Prague. Its 79 rooms were refurbished in 2002 with elegant dark wood and cream furnishings. The best views are from the eighth floor.

The Grand Mark Prague
MAP G3 ▪ Hybernská 12 ▪ 226 226111 ▪ www. grandmark.cz ▪ ⓀⓀⓀ
Once the Baroque Palace U Věžníků, the hotel offers an appealing blend of the historical and the contemporary. The rooms and suites are comfortable. Amenities include a spa

and wellness centre, as well as conference rooms. There is a gorgeous garden and terrace open all summer for dining.

Hotel Paříž
MAP P3 ▪ U Obecního domu 1 ▪ 222 195195 ▪ www.hotel-paris.cz ▪ Ⓚ Ⓚ Ⓚ
Built in 1904, this Art Nouveau treasure with its stunning staircase retains all its original charm while incorporating modern amenities such as heated bathroom floors and king-size beds in all rooms. The Royal Tower Suite has a spectacular 360° view.

Mandarin Oriental
MAP C3 ▪ Nebovidská 1 ▪ 233 088888 ▪ www.mandarinoriental.com/prague ▪ Ⓚ Ⓚ Ⓚ
The hotel is in a restored Dominican monastery. Its spa is in the former chapel and several of its 99 rooms have views over the city to Prague Castle.

The Mozart
MAP K6 ▪ Karolíny Světlé 34 ▪ 234 705111 ▪ www.themozart.com ▪ Ⓚ Ⓚ Ⓚ
Located on the waterfront, the Mozart offers spectacular views. Rooms are luxuriously over the top, with frescoes, chapel ceilings, architectural gems and medieval decor, fittings and fixtures.

Old Town Hotels

Hotel Liliová
MAP K5 ▪ Liliová 18 ▪ www.hotelliliova.com ▪ Ⓚ
Located just around the corner from Charles Bridge, this lovely guesthouse in a historic Prague building provides visitors with a quiet and comfortable place to stay.

Hotel Aurus
MAP K5 ▪ Karlova 3 ▪ 222 220262 ▪ www.prague residences.com/en/Aurus-Hotel ▪ Ⓚ Ⓚ
You'll tell the folks back home about this one. Set in the heart of Prague, this family-run four-star property is a beautiful historical monument protected by UNESCO. Exuding old-world charm, rooms are distinctive and have antique furnishings. Charles Bridge and the Old Town Square are only a short walk away.

Hotel Clementin
MAP K4 ▪ Seminářská 4 ▪ 222 231520 ▪ www.clementin.cz ▪ Ⓚ Ⓚ
The Clementin has the honour of being Prague's narrowest preserved building. The nine rooms in this Gothic edifice are small, but pleasant. You might struggle with large luggage.

Hotel Cloister Inn
MAP K6 ▪ Konviktská 14 ▪ 224 211020 ▪ www.cloisterinnhotel.com ▪ Ⓚ Ⓚ
The Jesuits founded the cloister, in 1660, that gives the hotel its name. It was then home to the Grey Sisters of St Francis, who were displaced by the secret police. The complex was returned to them in 1990. All 74 rooms have modern amenities.

Hotel Josef
MAP N2 ▪ Rybná 20 ▪ 221 700111 ▪ www.hoteljosef.com ▪ Ⓚ Ⓚ
Modern and trendy, this designer hotel fits in with Prague's urban chic image with its simple, clean-cut white and glass interiors and spacious rooms. The two buildings are connected by a courtyard, offering unique design elements. The lobby is a showpiece in itself. There is a stylish hotel bar, plus a fitness room and sauna. Visitors can sign up for a morning sightseeing jog.

Hotel Metamorphis
MAP M3 ▪ Týn 10 ▪ 221 771011 ▪ www.metamorphis.cz ▪ Ⓚ Ⓚ
Stylish touches, such as parquet floors and tiled stoves, and stirring views of the Ungelt courtyard and St James set this place apart. The patio restaurant is especially popular in the summer. There is no lift available.

Hotel U staré paní
MAP L5 ▪ Michalská 9 ▪ 224 228090 ▪ No air conditioning ▪ www.hotelustarepani.cz ▪ Ⓚ Ⓚ
A no-frills modern affair, staffed with an amiable crew. All 17 rooms have a minibar and satellite TV, but for better entertainment, catch the acts at the club below.

Lippert
MAP M3 ▪ Mikulášská 2 ▪ 224 232250 ▪ www.lipperthotel.cz ▪ Ⓚ Ⓚ
Across the street from Franz Kafka's birthplace, with views of St Nicholas and Týn churches, the Black Fox building is listed as a UNESCO World Cultural Heritage Site. There are only 12 rooms available, so book well in advance.

U Medvídků
MAP L6 ▪ Na Perštýně 7
▪ No air conditioning
▪ www.umedvidku.cz
▪ ⓚⓚ

Not only is "At the Small Bears" centrally located, it is also close to tram and metro stations. Connected to a historic brewery, it is set above the city's favourite Budvar pub. The rooms are charming, with Gothic rafters and Renaissance painted ceilings.

Monastery Garden
MAP N1 ▪ Řásnovka 783
▪ 222 311230 ▪ www. monasterygarden prague.com ▪ ⓚⓚⓚ

The elegantly appointed rooms embrace their 13th-century character. Wandering through the stairs and hallways, you might think you're in an Escher print. There is a small wellness club and excellent restaurant.

The President
MAP L1 ▪ Náměstí Curieových 1 ▪ 234 614100 ▪ www.axxos hotels.com ▪ ⓚⓚⓚ

This hotel is in a great location on the bank of the Vltava, close to the Josefov synagogues *(see p108)* and the St Agnes of Bohemia Convent *(see p109)*. The rooms are stylish and many have city or river views. Relax in the spa after a long day of sightseeing.

Malá Strana and Hradčany Hotels

Design Hotel Neruda Prague
MAP B2 ▪ Nerudova 225
▪ 257 535557 ▪ www. designhotelneruda.com
Set within a 14th-century building (once the home of Jan Neruda himself), this stylish boutique hotel has individually designed rooms, a great brunch café and even a small spa.

Hotel Čertovka
MAP D2 ▪ U lužického semináře 2 ▪ 257 011500
▪ www.certovka.cz ▪ ⓚⓚ

You can watch boats pass beneath Charles Bridge on the Čertovka canal from windows overlooking Prague's "Little Venice". Top-floor rooms have views of Prague castle. Parking is some distance from the hotel, however.

Hotel U Bílé lilie
MAP B3 ▪ Jánský vršek 4
▪ 732 538320 ▪ No air conditioning ▪ www. ubilelilie.cz ▪ ⓚⓚ

"At the White Lily" is situated close to Prague Castle and occupies a Renaissance building dating back to 1654. The hotel offers comfortable rooms in a quiet Malá Strana location.

Hotel Waldstein
MAP C2 ▪ Valdštejnské náměstí 6 ▪ 222 929390
▪ www.hotelwaldstein.cz
▪ ⓚⓚ

Adjoining Duke Albrecht von Wallenstein's palace on a quiet courtyard, this cozy hotel has 19 rooms and suites with modern design furniture. All the rooms are very comfortable and are furnished with a variety of antiques and reproductions.

U Tří Pštrosů
MAP D3 ▪ Dražického náměstí 12 ▪ 257 288888
▪ www.utripstrosu.cz
▪ ⓚⓚ

"At the Three Ostriches" gets its name from a 16th-century owner who was a purveyor of ostrich feathers. The rooms are comfortable and very quiet given their proximity to Charles Bridge.

Vintage Design Hotel Sax
MAP B3 ▪ Jánský vršek 3
▪ 775 859694 ▪ www.sax. cz ▪ ⓚⓚ

Tucked into the heart of Malá Strana, the modern Sax is close to the Church of Our Lady Victorious, St Nicholas Church, and Prague Castle. Decked out in 1950s, 1960s and 1970s style, the 25 rooms arranged around a central atrium are simple yet cozy.

Zlatá Hvězda
MAP C2 ▪ Nerudova 48
▪ 257 532867 ▪ www. hotelgoldenstar.cz ▪ ⓚⓚ

Built as the residence of Hradčany's mayor in 1372, the Golden Star has a long history of elegance. The apartments and rooms have period furniture and modern baths. Room No. 33 is sublime.

Aria
MAP C3 ▪ Tržiště 9 ▪ 225 334111 ▪ www.ariahotel. net ▪ ⓚⓚⓚ

Each of the themed rooms here is dedicated to a musical legend, be it Mozart or Dizzy Gillespie. The hotel's Coda Restaurant *(see p99)* ranks among Prague's best fine dining establishments. Guests have private access to the adjacent Vrtba Garden *(see p60)*.

Augustine
MAP D2 ▪ Letenská 12/33 ▪ 266 112233
▪ www.augustine hotel.com ▪ ⓚⓚⓚ

Sited in the 13th-century Augustinian monastery

of St Thomas, this luxury hotel offers rooms and suites (some created by combining the monks' cells) with Cubist-style furnishings popular in Prague in the 1920s and 1930s. There's a restaurant set in the cellar of the original St Thomas Brewery.

Biskupský dům
MAP D3 ■ Dražického náměstí 6 ■ 257 532320 ■ www.hotelbishops house.cz ■ ⓀⓀⓀ

The Bishop's House hotel occupies two buildings: one is the former residence of the bishop of Prague and the other was a butcher's shop in the 18th century. Between them are 45 rooms, all of which are very comfortable and taste-fully furnished.

Hotel Savoy
MAP A2 ■ Keplerova 6 ■ 224 302122 ■ www.savoyprague.cz ■ ⓀⓀⓀ

With stylishly designed suites and rooms, this four-star hotel is located a short walk from Prague Castle and Strahov Monastery. The hotel also features a wellness centre with a Finnish sauna, whirlpool and fitness area.

New Town Hotels

Novoměstský Hotel
MAP F5 ■ Řeznická 4 ■ 221 419911 ■ No air conditioning ■ www.novomestskyhotel.cz ■ Ⓚ

A bit old-fashioned, but the staff are helpful. Close to Karlovo náměstí and the New Town Hall.

Hotel 16 U Sv. Kateřiny
MAP F6 ■ Kateřinská 16 ■ 776 245960 ■ www.hotel16.cz ■ ⓀⓀ

The apartments and rooms at the luxuriously furnished St Catherine's are great value. Set near the river and the Prague Botanical Garden, this family-run inn is quiet, with charming eccen-tricities like the display of lovely junk from the next-door bazaar.

Hotel Adria
MAP N6 ■ Václavské náměstí 26 ■ 221 081111 ■ www.adria.cz ■ ⓀⓀ

Carmelite nuns serving at the Church of Our Lady of the Snows had their convent here in the 14th century. The 89 snug rooms look out either on the Franciscan Gardens or Wenceslas Square. Guarded parking nearby.

Hotel Grandium
MAP P6 ■ Politických vězňů 12 ■ 234 100100 ■ www.hotel-grandium.cz ■ ⓀⓀ

Designed with luxury in mind, the 365 rooms have fresh, contemporary decor. The hotel's sum-mer terrace and the light airy feel provide a distinct difference from other offerings in the area.

Hotel Icon
MAP F4 ■ V jámě 6 ■ 221 634100 ■ www.iconhotel.eu ■ ⓀⓀ

This hip boutique hotel has natural handmade beds from Sweden. An all-day breakfast, docks for smartphones in each room, complimentary Rituals toiletries and a massage centre are just some of the extras.

Hotel Jalta
MAP N6 ■ Václavské náměstí 45 ■ 222 822111 ■ www.hoteljalta.com ■ ⓀⓀⓀ

This Wenceslas Square designer hotel offers 94 stylish rooms and five luxurious suites. The Como restaurant serves excellent Mediterranean cuisine. There is also a casino, a fitness centre and a business centre.

Hotel Jungmann
MAP M6 ■ Jungmannovo náměstí 2 ■ 224 219501 ■ www.hotel-jungmann.cz ■ ⓀⓀ

This charming hotel is situated in a narrow house in Prague near Wenceslas Square and other sights of interest. It has 12 en-suite double rooms, each with Wi-Fi and air conditioning. Parking is arranged on request.

Hotel Opera
MAP H1 ■ Těšnov 13 ■ 222 315609 ■ www.hotel-opera.cz ■ ⓀⓀ

Built in the 1800s, Hotel Opera features a striking Neo-Renaissance façade. Centrally located, this hotel has 67 stylishly furnished rooms, some even have balconies with great city views.

Art Deco Imperial Hotel
MAP G2 ■ Na Poříčí 15 ■ 246 011663 ■ www.hotel-imperial.cz ■ ⓀⓀⓀ

This hotel is aimed at leisure and business trav-ellers who prefer the intimacy and individual approach of a boutique hotel. Modern technology and comforts combine seamlessly with the ori-ginal Art Deco interiors.

For a key to hotel price categories see p140

Carlo IV Prague
MAP G3 ■ Senovážné námestí 13 ■ 224 593111 ■ www.dahotels.com ■ ⓚⓚⓚ
Close to the main train station, this elegant hotel has Italian opulence, efficient staff and an impressive spa. Make sure you opt for the breakfast package – it is well worth the extra cost.

Hotel Palace
MAP N5 ■ Panská 12 ■ 224 093181 ■ www. palacehotel.cz ■ ⓚⓚⓚ
As classy as the hotels around the corner on Wenceslas Square, the Art Nouveau hotel is renowned for its excellent service. It offers several packages, including a two-day honeymoon deal, complete with tours and other extras. Little luxuries include marble-lined bathrooms.

Majestic Plaza
MAP F5 ■ Štepánská 33 ■ 221 486100 ■ www. hotel-majestic.cz ■ ⓚⓚⓚ
This popular hotel is set in two interconnected buildings, one of which was where writer Jaroslav Hašek (see p50) was born. Biedermeier and Art Deco style rooms are on offer, along with great views from the seventh floor.

Hostels

Ahoy! Hostel
MAP L6 ■ Na Perštýně 10 ■ 773 004003 ■ No air conditioning ■ www. ahoyhostel.com ■ ⓚ
Set in a 17th-century building, this hostel offers private and dormitory rooms which have been beautified by local street artists. The hostel provides a clean and safe environment with friendly staff, free Wi-Fi and a fully equipped kitchen.

MeetMe23
MAP G4 ■ Washingtonova 23 ■ 601 023023 ■ www. meetme23.com ■ ⓚ
This stylish boutique hostel near Prague's main train station offers a choice of beds in mixed and female dorms. Private rooms and apartments for between one and four people are also available. The restaurant, Meat Beer, has swiftly become a backpacker favourite.

Czech Inn
MAP C6 ■ Francouzská 76, Vršovice ■ 210 011 100 ■ No air conditioning ■ www. czech-inn.com ■ ⓚ
This hostel features a chic interior and various room options, including private en-suite rooms, dorm rooms and apartments with kitchen facilities. A breakfast buffet is available for an additional cost. There is also a café and a bar on site.

Brix Hostel
MAP B6 ■ Roháčova 15, Žižkov ■ 731 126100 ■ www.brixhostel.com ■ ⓚ
This hostel, in the heart of pub-filled Žižkov, is popular for its large communal terrace, complete with a ping-pong table.

Hostel ELF
MAP H3 ■ Husitská 11 ■ 222 540963 ■ No air conditioning ■ www. hostelelf.com ■ ⓚ
On the second floor of a fin de siècle building near the main bus and train stations, Hostel ELF's rooms range from singles to 12-bed dorms. There is a garden, shared kitchen and common room. The staff will arrange walking tours for you.

Hostel Strahov
MAP A4 ■ Vaníčkova 7, Strahov ■ 234 678111 ■ No air conditioning ■ recepce@suz.cvut.cz ■ ⓚ
The dorms provide student housing through the school year, although Block 12 is always open.

Old Prague Hostel
MAP N2 ■ Benediktská 2 ■ 731 559133 ■ No air conditioning ■ ⓚ
In central Prague, this hostel has two- to five-bed rooms and four- to twelve-bed dorms, some with private showers. There's a fully equipped kitchen and dining room, movie lounge and free internet access.

Sir Toby's Hostel
MAP B5 ■ Dělnická 24, Holešovice ■ 246 032611 ■ No air conditioning ■ www.sirtobys.com ■ ⓚ
The staff here go to great lengths to be hospitable, throwing the occasional barbecue and helping travellers find other accommodation when Sir Toby's is full. The baths, bedrooms and kitchen are immaculately clean.

Charles Bridge Economic Hostel
MAP D3 ■ Mostecká 4 ■ 257 213420 ■ www. charlesbridgehostel.com ■ ⓚⓚ
Located near Charles Bridge, this small charming property offers fully furnished

rooms equipped with a kitchen, TV, Wi-Fi, and free coffee. Free tours are available.

Miss Sophie's

MAP G6 ▪ Melounova 3 ▪ 210 011210 ▪ www. miss-sophies.com ▪ ⓚ ⓚⓚ
Located not far from the centre, this is an ideal base from which to explore the city. It offers dorms as well as private rooms with en-suite bathrooms. Slightly more expensive are the apartments, which come complete with a kitchen.

Pensions and B&Bs

Pension Karlova

MAP K4 ▪ Karlova 8 ▪ 606 259030 ▪ www. pensionkarlova.com
The location of this family-friendly Old Town pension, just a few steps from Charles Bridge, is unmatched. The rooms are a mix of doubles/twins, triples and quadruples. Though they are simply furnished, all rooms are spacious, clean and comfortable. Given its location, the pension itself does not provide any parking space but there are paid alternatives nearby.

Pension Dientzenhofer

MAP D3 ▪ Nosticova 2 ▪ 257 311319 ▪ www. pension-dientzenhofer. worhot.com ▪ ⓚ
This quiet house on the banks of the Čertovka canal is the birthplace of architect Kilian Ignaz Dientzenhofer, who built the nearby St Nicholas Church and other Baroque edifices. This famous pension

has shabby-chic rooms and an idyllic garden with river views.

Pension Kliská

MAP B5 ▪ Veltěžská 26 ▪ 284 687289 ▪ www. pensionkliska.cz ▪ ⓚ
This small guesthouse is situated in a quiet residential suburb of the city. The nearest metro station, Kobylisy (Line C), is a mere 5-minute walk away. From there, it is only five stops to bustling Wenceslas Square in the heart of town.

Pension Jana

MAP C6 ▪ Dykova 20, Vinohrady ▪ 222 511777 ▪ www.dhotels.cz
This four-storey Vinohrady villa turned no-frills pension offers a mix of budget bedrooms with shared facilities and more spacious rooms with private bathrooms. There's also a lovely garden. It's just a short walk from Jiřího z Poděbrad metro station.

Pension Beta

MAP B6 ▪ Jaromírova 46, Nusle ▪ 222 564385 ▪ www.pensionbeta.cz
A good budget option in a less-visited corner of Prague, this Nusle pension offers basic but comfortable bedrooms and easy tram connections to the city centre. It's also just a short (if steep) walk to Vyšehrad.

3 Epoques

MAP K5 ▪ Řetězová 3 ▪ 222 743781 ▪ www. pragueresidences.com ▪ ⓚ ⓚ
This hotel is housed in the oldest building, a 12th-century Roman

palace that was home to Jiří z Poděbrad (King George) in the 15th century. There are eight large and fully furnished, luxury apartments.

Dům u Velké Boty

MAP B3 ▪ Vlašská 30 ▪ 257 532088 ▪ www. dumuvelkeboty.cz ▪ ⓚ ⓚ
Dům u Velké boty or the "House at the Big Boot" is a small family hotel in an old Renaissance burgher house in Malá Strana. The rooms have modern amenities as well as genuine period furniture, lights and decor. Each room is different in size, type and ambience.

Red Chair Hotel

MAP K5 ▪ Liliová 4 ▪ 296 180018 ▪ No air conditioning ▪ www. redchairhotel.site ▪ ⓚ ⓚ
Located in a building dating from the 15th century, the Red Chair hotel offers clean and comfortable rooms with big bathrooms. A simple and tasty breakfast is available.

U Raka

MAP A2 ▪ Černínská 10 ▪ 220 511100 ▪ www. hoteluraka.cz ▪ ⓚ ⓚ
Perhaps Prague's most romantic address, "At the Crayfish" started out as a barn in 1739. Inside its log walls today are some charming country-style rooms. Room No. 6 has its own private garden, fireplace and a well. Located close to the Prague Castle and Loreta. Children over the age of 12 are welcome here.

For a key to hotel price categories see p140

Apartments

Apartments U Císaře
MAP B6 ▪ Slezská 23, Vinohrady ▪ 233 920118 ▪ No air conditioning ▪ www.hotelsprague.cz/ucisare ▪ ⓚ

This booking agency offers six apartments in an 1885 building located near the metro and tram stop Jiřího z Poděbrad, two stops from Wenceslas Square. There are fully equipped kitchens, TVs and a basement restaurant. The cost includes bed linen and utilities.

Appia Hotel Residences
MAP B3 ▪ Šporkova 3 ▪ 257 215819 ▪ No air conditioning ▪ www.appiaresidences prague.cz ▪ ⓚⓚ

This appealing Malá Strana residence has a mix of hotel-style suites and spacious private apartments. An original 12th-century breakfast hall and a lovely courtyard garden add to its charm.

4 Arts Apartments
MAP N3 ▪ Rybná 3 ▪ 222 743781 ▪ www.pragueresidences.com

Located between the Old Town Square and Powder Gate, these 15 designer apartments vary from studios all the way up to three-bedroom options. Each includes king-size beds and fully equipped kitchens.

Cathedral Prague Apartments
MAP M3 ▪ Týnská 625 ▪ 735 008989 ▪ www.cathedral-prague-apartments.com

Just a few steps from the Old Town Square,

this group of 13 studios and apartments offer quick respite from the area's crowds. Note that only deluxe apartments come with kitchenettes for self catering.

Hunger Wall Residence
MAP C4 ▪ Plaská 8 ▪ 257 404040 ▪ No air conditioning ▪ www.hungerwall-residence.com ▪ ⓚ

This early 20th-century renovated building, with elements of Art Nouveau architecture, offers 18 stylish and richly furnished apartments each with individual design.

Residence Bene
MAP P3 ▪ Dlouhá 48 ▪ 222 313171 ▪ www.residence-bene.cz ▪ ⓚ

Set in the historical heart of Prague, the cozy apartments at Bene are a great alternative to a traditional hotel stay. The Palladium Shopping Centre is a short distance away.

Lazenska N°4
MAP D3 ▪ Lázeňská 4 ▪ 233 920118 ▪ www.lazenska4.com

You'll find this Baroque palace turned boutique residence on a quiet Malá Strana street, just around the corner from Lennon Wall. It features 14 fully-serviced, high-end apartments, which are suitable for three to six people.

Mooo Apartments
MAP E5 ▪ Myslíkova 22, Praha 2 ▪ 608 278422 ▪ www.mooo-apartments.com ▪ ⓚⓚ

These stylish and luxurious apartments marry slick urban

design with cozy countryside ambience, and are perfect for a design-conscious traveller. They have kitchenettes equipped with the latest Bosch appliances, designer bathrooms, concierge services, high-speed Wi-Fi and some have balconies with magnificent views of the city.

Salvator Apartments
MAP M3 ▪ Dušní 6 ▪ 224 990990 ▪ ⓚⓚ

Situated in the historical centre of the city in a quiet area near St Salvator Church, Salvator offers three apartments fully equipped with modern furniture and amenities such as air conditioning or safe box. Pets are allowed on request.

Mordecai 12 Apartments
MAP L3 ▪ Maiselova 12 ▪ 222 743781 ▪ www.pragueresidences.com

Stay in the heart of Prague's Jewish Quarter at one of these 12 modern apartments. You can opt for a basic studio with a kitchenette or splash out on a two-bedroom apartment with a terrace and fully equipped kitchen.

Hotels Outside the City Centre

Hotel Belvedere
MAP B5 ▪ Milady Horákové 19, Holešovice ▪ 220 106111 ▪ No air conditioning ▪ www.hotelbelvedere prague.cz ▪ ⓚ

Located near the Trade Fair Palace (Veletržní Palace), the Belvedere is a short walk to the Old Town or Prague Castle. Trams stop just outside. The rooms are very comfortable for the price.

Hotel Excellent

Líbeznická 19, Kobylisy ▪ **284 687295** ▪ **No air conditioning** ▪ **www. hotel-excellent.cz** ▪ Ⓚ
This small hotel lives up to its name if you don't mind being away from the crowd. Your hosts are happy to book flights, train tickets or seats at the opera, or just show you around town.

Corinthia Prague

MAP B6 ▪ **Kongresová 1, Vyšehrad** ▪ **261 191211** ▪ **www.corinthia.com/ prague** ▪ ⓀⓀ
Located just a short walk from Tabor Gate (which marks the entrance to Vyšehrad Citadel), this high-rise hotel is part of the luxury hotel chain Corinthia. It's known for its modern interiors, a good choice of restaurants and an appealing rooftop pool and spa (which has stunning views of the city below). Corinthia Prague is especially popular with business travellers, thanks to its proximity to the Congress Centre; it's also just a five-minute metro ride from Wenceslas Square.

Ibis Mala Strana

Plzeňská 14, Smíchov ▪ **221 701700** ▪ **www.all. accor.com** ▪ Ⓚ
A no-nonsense hotel with modern amenities and a devotion to customer service. Rooms are small and comfort-

able. This is a good choice for travellers who don't want to spend a lot of time sitting around.

Akcent Hotel

MAP A6 ▪ **Stroupež-nického 1, Smíchov** ▪ **257 003494** ▪ **www. akcent-hotel.cz** ▪ ⓀⓀ
This modern three-star hotel has splendid views of Prague from all 53 of its rooms. It is located on the seventh floor of a 1930s Functionalist-style office building.

Botanique Hotel

Sokolovská 11, Karlín ▪ **226 222600** ▪ **www. hotelbotanique.com** ▪ ⓀⓀ
Situated near the Florenc metro station, this inn offers 214 rooms with soft beds, well-lit work areas, en-suite bathrooms, safes, mini fridges and flat screen TVs. A coffee bar and a fitness and wellness centre are on site. Conference facilities are available.

Don Giovanni Prague

MAP B6 ▪ **Vinohradská 157a, Žižkov** ▪ **267 031111** ▪ **www.hotel-giovanni.cz** ▪ ⓀⓀ
The Don Giovanni offers 376 elegant rooms and 35 suites. Hotel guests can take advantage of the spa treatment facilities and the babysitting service. Conveniently located near metro, bus and tram stops.

Hotel Anna

MAP B6 ▪ **Budečská 17** ▪ **222 513111** ▪ **No air conditioning** ▪ **www. hotelanna.cz** ▪ ⓀⓀ
The Art Nouveau building in a quiet Vinohrady location was built as

a private residence in the 19th century. The hotel's 26 rooms are painted in beautiful pastel shades and decorated with engravings of historic Prague. The top-floor suites enjoy views of the castle and the Old Town. There's a beautiful breakfast room.

Vienna House

MAP A5 ▪ **Evropská 15, Dejvice** ▪ **296 559111** ▪ **www.viennahouse. com** ▪ ⓀⓀ
Near, but not within earshot of the airport, this hotel has 400 rooms. Facilities include several restaurants, a business centre and a spa and a wellness area. Children under six stay for free. There's good access to the centre.

Hotel Julián

MAP A6 ▪ **Elišky Peškové 11, Smíchov** ▪ **257 311144** ▪ **www.hotel julian.com** ▪ ⓀⓀ
Within walking distance of Malá Strana, the Julián is an Art Nouveau charmer, with red-velvet lift and a fireside library. Some suites have a kitchen and there is a business centre.

Hotel Le Palais

MAP B6 ▪ **U Zvonařky 1, Vinohrady** ▪ **234 634111** ▪ **www.lepalaishotel.eu** ▪ ⓀⓀⓀ
One of Prague's finest examples of *belle époque* architecture, this former residential building from 1841 is now a boutique hotel with plush rooms, a spa and wellness centre and a library. There is also a fine dining restaurant.

For a key to hotel price categories see p140

General Index

Acknowledgments

This edition updated by

Contributor Joseph Reaney
Senior Editors Alison McGill, Dipika Dasgupta
Senior Art Editor Stuti Tiwari
Project Editors Lucy Sara-Kelly, Anuroop Sanwalia
Art Editor Bandana Paul
Assistant Editor Nandini Desiraju
Picture Research Administrator Vagisha Pushp
Picture Research Manager Taiyaba Khatoon
Publishing Assistant Halima Mohammed
Jacket Designer Jordan Lambley
Senior Cartographer Subhashree Bharati
Cartography Manager Suresh Kumar
Senior DTP Designer Tanveer Zaidi
Senior Production Editor Jason Little
Senior Production Controller Kariss Ainsworth
Managing Editors Shikha Kulkarni, Beverly Smart, Hollie Teague
Managing Art Editor Sarah Snelling
Senior Managing Art Editor Priyanka Thakur
Art Director Maxine Pedliham
Publishing Director Georgina Dee

DK would like to thank the following for their contribution to the previous editions: Theodore Schwinke, Mark Baker, Helen Peters, Eddie Gerald, Frantisek Preucil, Jiri Dolezal, Jiri Kopriva, Nigel Hudson, Rough Guides/Eddie Gerald, Rough Guides/Jon Cunningham, Rough Guides/Natascha Sturny, Peter Wilson, Stanislav Tereba, Vladimir Kozlik.

The publisher would like to thank the following for their kind permission to reproduce their photographs:

Key: a-above; b-below/bottom; c-centre; f-far; l-left; r-right; t-top

123RF.com: Ozgur Guven 14br; tich 37cra.
4Corners: SIME/Stefano Cellai 2tl, 8–9.
Alamy Stock Photo: AA World Travel Library 119cl; Radim Beznoska 42bc, 54c, 81tr; Home Bird 71tr; B.O'Kane 116clb; Petr Bonek 16br; David Cole 50tl; David Crausby 20cb; CTK 50bl, /Hajsky Libor 43clb, /Kestner Karel 51tl; DPA Picture Alliance 51clb; FineArt 50cr, 59tr; Eddie Gerald 62cr; Hemis.fr /Christophe Boisvieux 15b; Heritage Image Partnership Ltd /Fine Art Images 50br, 51tr; Images & Stories 4crb; Images-Europa 64t; Ivoha 80t; isifa Image service s.r.o./Landisch; Berger Jiří 38clb; Brenda Kean 102ca; John Kellerman 62bl, 103cla, Loop Images / Anna Stowe 79cl, Ivan Marchuk 28crb; mauritius images GmbH /Cash 36br; Hercules Milas 93br; Mira 97tr; Stefano Paterna 122tl; PBarchive 15cl; Pegaz 60t; 117cla; PhotoBliss 95bl; J. Pie 61tl, 77b, 120tl; PjrTravel 53tr, 86tc; Prisma Archivo 32br; Profimedia.CZ a.s. /Michaela Dusikova 63bl, 86cra; REDA &CO srl / Federico Meneghetti 30cl; Sergi Reboredo 91cla; Simon Reddy 70tl; Shannon99 18cla; Anna Vaczi 71clb; VPC Photo 42tl, 45crb; Terence Waeland 11cra; Mike Withers 58bl.
Ambiente: 99clb, 113cl.
Aromi: 129tl.
Artel Glass: 76cl.
Bakeshop Praha: 112tr.
Bridgeman Images: Narodni Galerie, Prague/St. Matthew, from the chapel of Karlstejn Castle (c.1365) Theodoricus of Prague 34bl, /Resurrection of Christ (c.1350) Master of the Cycle of Vyssi Brod (tempera on panel) 34–5, /The Resurrection (c.1380) Master of

the Trebon Altarpiece tempera on panel 35tl, /Martyrdom of St, Florian (1516) by Albrecht Altdorfer 35cb; De Agostini Picture Library/A. Dagli Orti 42cra.

Café Kafíčko: 98cla.

Český porcelán: Foto Studio H 88bc.

Corbis: Michele Falzone 45b.

DepositPhotos Inc: Da Liu 93t.

DOX: Jan Slavik 126crb.

Dreamstime.com: Abxyz 106–7; Andrey Andronov 86b, David Bailey 23cr; Ryhor Bruyeu 18crb, 94tl; Neacsu Razvan Chirnoaga 36cla; Cividin 94crb; Sorin Colac 26cl, 52tl, 85tl; Ionut David 38–9; Debu55y 65br; Delstudio 19c, 84tl; Pavel Dospiva 37clb; Dragoneye 6cb; Viorel Dudau 77cl; Tatiana Dyuvbanova 36–7c; Emicristea 12cla; Frenta 4cla; Marian Garai 127ca, 127br; GoneWithTheWind 3tl, 12crb, 82–3; Gornostaj 2tr, 40–41; Diego Grandi 59b; Grounder 102b; Nataliya Hora 24–5; Jakatics 101tl; Jorisvo 43tr; Kajanek 19tl; Olena Korol 101br; Daniel Korzeniewski 85br; Edward Lemery Iii 23bc; Miroslav Liska 16–17; Lorpic99 28–9; Marietf 10ca; Marina99 10clb, 78br; Martinslezacek 114cl; Mikhail Markovskiy 123tl; Krisztian Miklosy 13crb; Mirekdeml 60b; Martin Molcan 3tr, 12–13, 130–31; Chris Moncrieff 17cr; Nomadbeg 92tl; Filip Odráška 70b; Olgacov 56–7; Ploutarxina 10crb; Pytycech 10cla; Juha Remes 30b; Radomír Režný 23tl, 37tr; Saky13 46clb; Tatiana Savvateeva 87tl; Konstantin Semenov 22bl; Oleksii Sergieiev 87bl; Slowcentury 61tr; Krzysztof Slusarczyk 95tl; Radovan Smokon 31br; Igor Stevanovic 39tl, 44clb; Alyaksandr Stzhalkouski 16cla, 18bc; Andrey Tarantin 4cl; Tavi79 7cr; Thecriss 60cr, 114br; Thinkart 110cr; Tomas1111 6cla, 10–11, 22–3; Uko_jesita 22br; David Pereiras Villagrá 20cla, 111bl; Vodickap 92tl; Richard Van Der Woude 11tl, 14tr, 109tl; Wrangel 53b, 76tr, 81clb; Yuri4u80 125bl; Yykkaa 13clb.

Field Restaurant: 73tr.

Getty Images: Archive Photos 28cl; Corbis Historical / Fine Art 33crb; Heritage Images 32–3; Wasin Pummarin / EyeEm 1.

Grand Café Orient: Jaroslav Turek 75clb.

Hemingway Bar: 75tr.

Hotel U Prince: 90bl.

iStockphoto.com: coramueller 39cra; GoneWithTheWindStock 29bl; scanrai 4cla; Vladislav Zoloto 115tr.

John Lennon Pub: 98br.

Karel Zeman Museum: Libor Svacek 63tl.

King Solomon Restaurant: 113br.

Kuchyň: 105cr.

La Degustation: 72cla.

Laterna Magika: Petr Našic Jeseniova 66b.

Lobkowicz Palace Museum and Café: 12bl,104b.

Loreto Sanctuary: 26br, 27clb, 27crb, 27bc.

Lucerna Music Bar: 69br.

Mary Evans Picture Library: INTERFOTO/Bildarchiv Hansmann 61cl.

Moser Glassworks: 88cla.

Mysteria Pragensia: 54t.

Národní Muzeum: 48tr, 48cl, 125tl, 126tl.

National Gallery Prague: 32clb.

National Technical Museum: 49br.

National Theatre Opera and State Opera: 66cla, 67tl.

Obchod vším možným: 97clb.

Pivovarský dům Benedict: 74br.

Ponec: 66bl.

Prague Spring Festival: Ivan Maly 79tr.

Radost FX: 68tl.

Restaurace Pastička: 128br.

Robert Harding Picture Library: Godong 4clb; Fraser Hall 4t; Henryk T. Kaiser 11crb; Raimund Kutter 26–7; Martin Moxter 4b; Alexander Poschel 4cra; Phil Robinson 19br; Travel Pix 11clb; Kimberly Walker 18–19.

Roxy: 89tr; Marek Podhora 68bl.

SaSaZu, Prague: Adi Gilad 68cr.

Shutterstock.com: Str / EPA 80br.

Stefanik Observatory: 39crb.

Studio Šperk: 112bc.

SuperStock: age fotostock/Christian Goupi 67br; imageBROKER 21cb.

Terasa U Zlaté studně: 99tr.

Trade Fair Palace: 11tc.

U Fleků: 74cla, 120crb.

U Šumavy: 121crb.

Vagon Club: 89bl.

Wallenstein Palace: 96clb.

Zatisiclub: 72b.

Zone: 119br.

Zoo Praha: Petr Hamerni ík 65br.

Cover images

Front and spine: **Getty Images:** Wasin Pummarin / EyeEm.

Back: **Alamy Stock Photo:** Hercules Milas cl, George Oze tr; **Dreamstime. com:** Ekaterinabelova crb; Veronika Galkina tl; **Getty Images:** Wasin Pummarin / EyeEm b.

Pull out map cover image

Wasin Pummarin / EyeEm.

All other images © Dorling Kindersley

For further information see: www.dkimages.com

Illustrator Chris Orr & Associates.

Commissioned Photography First edition created by Sargasso Media Ltd, London.

Penguin
Random
House

First Edition 2003

Published in Great Britain by
Dorling Kindersley Limited,
DK, One Embassy Gardens, 8 Viaduct
Gardens, London SW11 7BW, UK

The authorised representative in the EEA is
Dorling Kindersley Verlag GmbH. Arnulfstr.
124, 80636 Munich, Germany

Published in the United States by
DK Publishing, 1745 Broadway, 20th Floor,
New York, NY 10019, USA

Copyright © 2003, 2023
DorlingKindersley Limited
A Penguin Random House Company

23, 24, 25, 26 10 9 8 7 6 5 4 3 2 1

The publishers cannot accept responsibility
for any consequences arising from the use
of this book, nor for any material on third
party websites, and cannot guarantee that
any website address in this book will be
a suitable source of travel information.

A CIP catalogue record is available
from the British Library.

A catalogue record for this book is available
from the Library of Congress.

ISSN 1479-344X

ISBN 978-0-2416-2123-3

Printed and bound in Malaysia

www.dk.com

*As a guide to abbreviations in visitor information
blocks:* **Adm** = *admission charge;* **D** = *dinner.*

MIX
Paper | Supporting
responsible forestry
FSC™ C018179

Phrase Book

In an Emergency

Help!	Pomoc!	po-mots
Stop!	Zastavte!	zas-tav-te
Call a doctor!	Zavolejte doktora!	za-vo-ley-te dok-to-ra!
Call an ambulance!	Zavolejte sanitku!	za-vo-ley-te sa-nit-ku!
Call the police!	Zavolejte policii!	za-vo-ley-te poli-tsi-yi!
Call the fire brigade!	Zavolejte hasiče	za-vo-ley-te ha-si-che
Where is the telephone?	Kde je telefon?	gde ye te-le-fohn?
the nearest hospital?	nejbližší nemocnice?	ney-blizh-shee ne-mo-tsnyi-tse?

Communication Essentials

Yes/No	Ano/Ne	ano/ne
Please	Prosím	pro-seem
Thank you	Děkuji vám	dye-ku-ji vahm
Excuse me	Prosím vás	pro-seem vahs
Hello	Dobrý den	do-bree den
Goodbye	Na shledanou	na shle-da-nou
Good evening	Dobrý večer	do-bree ve-cher
morning	ráno	rah-no
afternoon	odpoledne	od-po-led-ne
evening	večer	ve-cher
yesterday	včera	vche-ra
today	dnes	dnes
tomorrow	zítra	zee-tra
here	tady	ta-di
there	tam	tam
What?	Co?	tso?
When?	Kdy?	gdi?
Why?	Proč?	proch?
Where?	Kde?	gde?

Useful Phrases

How are you?	Jak se máte?	yak se mah-te?
Very well, thank you.	Velmi dobře děkuji	vel-mi do-brze dye-ku-yi
Pleased to meet you	Těší mě	tye-shee mnye
See you soon	Uvidíme se brzy	u-vi-dyee-me-se brzy
That's fine	To je v pořádku	to ye vpo-rzhahdku
Where is/are…?	Kde je/jsou …?	gde ye/ysou …?
How long does it take to get to…?	Jak dlouho to trvá se dostat do…?	yak dlou-ho to tr-vah se dos-tat …?
How do I get to…?	Jak se dostanu k …?	yak se dos-ta-nuh k…?
Do you speak English?	Mluvíte anglicky?	mlu-vee-te an-glits-ki?
I don't understand	Nerozumím	ne-ro-zu-meem
Could you speak more slowly?	Mohl(a)* byste mluvit trochu pomaleji?	mo-hl(a) bys-te mlu-vit tro-khu po-ma-ley?
Pardon?	Prosím?	pro-seem?
I'm lost	Ztratil(a)* jsem se	stra-tyil (a) ysem se

Sightseeing

art gallery	galerie	ga-le-ri-ye
church	kostel	kos-tel
garden	zahrada	za-hra-da
library	knihovna	knyi-hov-na
museum	muzeum	mu-ze-um
railway station	nádraží	nah-dra-zhee
tourist information	turistické informace	tu-ris-tits-ke in-for-ma-tse
closed for the public holiday	státní svátek	staht-nyee svah-tek

Shopping

How much does this cost?	Co to stojí?	tso to sto-yee?
I would like…	Chtěl(a)* bych…	khtyel(a) bikh…
Do you have…?	Máte…?	maa-te …?
I'm just looking	Jenom se dívám	ye-nom se dyee-vahm
Do you take credit cards?	Berete kreditní karty?	be-re-te kre-dit –nyee kar-ti?
What time do you open/ close?	V kolik otevíráte/ zavíráte?	v ko-lik o-te-vee-rah-te/ za-vee-rah-te?
this one	tento	ten-to
that one	tamten	tam-ten
expensive	drahý	dra-hee
cheap	levný	lev-nee
size	velikost	ve-li-kost
white	bílý	bee-lee
black	černý	cher-nee
red	červený	cher-ve-nee
yellow	žlutý	zhlu-tee
green	zelený	ze-le-nee
blue	modrý	mod-ree
brown	hnědý	hnye-dee

Types of Shop

bank	banka	ban-ka
bakery	pekárna	pe-kahr-na
butcher	řeznictví	rzhez-nyits-tvee
chemist (prescriptions etc)	lékárna	leh-kahr-na
chemist (toiletries etc)	drogerie	dro-ge-riye
delicatessen	lahůdky	la-hood-ki
grocery	potraviny	po-tra-vi-ni
glass	sklo	sklo
market	trh	trh
post office	pošta	posh-ta
supermarket	samoobsluha	sa-mo-ob-slu-ha
travel agency	cestovní kancelář	tses-tov-nyi kan-tse-laarzh

Staying in a Hotel

Do you have a vacant room?	Máte volný pokoj?	mah-te vol-nee po-koy?
double room	dvoulůžkový pokoj	dvou-loozh-ko-vee po-koy
with double bed	s dvojitou postelí	s dvoy-tou pos-te-lee
twin room	pokoj s dvěma postelemi	po-koy sdvye-ma pos-te-le-mi
porter	vrátný	vrah-tnee
I have a reservation	Mám reservaci	mahm re-zer-va-tsi

alternatives for a female speaker are shown in brackets

Eating Out

Have you got a table for…?	Máte stůl pro …?	mah-te stool pro …?
I'd like to reserve a table	Chtěl(a)* bych rezervovat stůl	khtyel(a) bikh re-zer-vo-vat stool
breakfast	snídaně	snyee-danye
lunch	oběd	ob-yed
dinner	večeře	ve-che-rzhe
The bill, please	Prosím, účet	pro-seem oo-chet
I am a vegetarian	Jsem vegetarián (ka)*	ysem veghe-tariahn(ka)
waitress!	slečno	slech-no
waiter!	pane vrchní!	pane vrkh-nyee!
fixed-price menu	standardní menu	stan-dard-nyee menu
dish of the day	nabídka dne	na-beed-ka dne
starter	předkrm	przhed-krm
main course	hlavní jídlo	hlav-nyee yeed-lo
vegetables	zelenina	ze-le-nyi-na
dessert	zákusek	zah-kusek
cover charge	poplatek	pop-la-tck
wine list	nápojový lístek	nah-po-yo-vee lees-tek
rare (steak)	krvavý	kr-va-vee
medium	středně udělaný	strzhed-nye u-dye-la-nee
well done	dobře udělaný	dobrzhe-u-dye-la-nee
glass	sklenice	sklen-yitse
bottle	láhev	lah-hev
knife	nůž	noozh
fork	vidlička	vid-lich-ka
spoon	lžíce	lzhee-tse

Menu Decoder

biftek	bif-tek	steak
bílé víno	bee-leh vee-no	white wine
bramborové knedlíky	bram-bo-ro-veh kne-dleeki	potato dumplings
brambory	bram-bo-ri	potatoes
chléb	khlehb	bread
cukr	tsukr	sugar
čaj	chay	tea
červené víno	cher-ven-eh vee-no	red wine
grilované	gril-ov-a-neh	grilled
houskové knedlíky	ho-sko-veh kne-dleeki	bread dumplings
hovězí	hov-ye-zee	beef
hranolky	hra-nol-ki	chips
husa	hu-sa	goose
jehněčí	ye-hnye-chee	lamb
kachna	kakh-na	duck
kapr	ka-pr	carp
káva	kah-va	coffee
kuře	ku-rzhe	chicken
kyselé zelí	kis-el-eh zel-ee	sauerkraut
maso	ma-so	meat
máslo	mah-slo	butter
mléko	mleh-ko	milk
mořská jídla	morzh-skah yeed-la	seafood
párek	paa-rek	sausage
pečený	petsh-en-eh	baked
pečené	pech-en-eh	roast
polévka	po-lehv-ka	soup
pivo	pi-vo	beer
ryba	ri-ba	fish
rýže	ree-zhe	rice
salát	sa-laat/sa-laht	salad
sůl	sool	salt
sýr	seer	cheese
šunka	shun-ka	ham
vařená/ uzená	va-rzhe-nah u-zenah	cooked smoked
telecí	te-le-tsee	veal
vajíčko	va-yeech-ko	egg
vařené	va-rzhe-neh	boiled
vepřové	vep-rzho-veh	pork
voda	vo-da	water
zelenina	ze-le-nyi-na	vegetables

Numbers

1	jedna	yed-na
2	dvě	dvye
3	tř	trzhi
4	čtyři	chti-rzhi
5	pět	pyet
6	šest	shest
7	sedm	sedm
8	osm	osm
9	devět	dev-yet
10	deset	de-set
11	jedenáct	ye-de-nahtst
12	dvanáct	dva-nahtst
13	třináct	trzhi-nahtst
14	čtrnáct	chtr-nahtst
15	patnáct	pat-nahtst
16	šestnáct	shest-nahtst
17	sedmnáct	sedm-nahtst
18	osmnáct	osm-nahtst
19	devatenáct	de-va-te-nahtst
20	dvacet	dva-tset
21	dvacet jedna	dva-tset yed-na
22	dvacet dva	dva-tset dva
30	třicet	trzhi-tset
40	čtyřicet	chti-rzhi-tset
50	padesát	pa-de-saht
60	šedesát	she-de-saht
70	sedmdesát	sedm-de-saht
80	osmdesát	osm-de-saht
90	devadesát	de-va-de-saht
100	sto	sto
1,000	tisíc	tyi-seets
2,000	dva tisíce	dva tyi-see-tse
5,000	pět tisíc	pyet tyi-seets
1,000,000	milión	mi-li-ohn

Time

one minute	jedna minuta	yed-na mi-nu-ta
one hour	jedna hodina	yed-na ho-dyi-na
half an hour	půl hodiny	pool ho-dyi-ni
day	den	den
week	týden	tee-den
Monday	pondělí	pon-dye-lee
Tuesday	úterý	oo-te-ree
Wednesday	středa	strzhe-da
Thursday	čtvrtek	chtvr-tek
Friday	pátek	pah-tek
Saturday	sobota	so-bo-ta
Sunday	neděle	ned-yel-e

*alternatives for a female speaker are shown in brackets